Bruce Morgan

BEATLES' SINGLES

AUSTIN MACAULEY PUBLISHERS™

LONDON · CAMBRIDGE · NEW YORK · SHARJAH

A CIP catalogue record for this title is available from the British Library.

ISBN 9781528912334 (Paperback)
ISBN 9781528960090 (ePub e-book)

www.austinmacauley.com

First Published (2020)
Austin Macauley Publishers Ltd
25 Canada Square
Canary Wharf
London
E14 5LQ

Table of Contents

Introduction

This is a purely reference guidebook for those people who collect Beatles' Singles. It lists all the 'Singles' record that were issued by them worldwide.

There are several types of manufactured singles available throughout the various countries of the world, played at three different speeds. i.e. 331/3, 45 and 78 RPM. These are listed under their playing speeds. The 45s being the most prolific of the three. 331/3 and 78s being for the more specialist collectors.

The book is laid out very simply by alphabetical order of title under their relevant speed.

It tells you the title and what is available on the 'flip side', i.e. Rock and Roll Music was released in a variety of countries with ten different flip sides. It informs you of the country of origin, the label that it was issued under, the label catalogue number, year of release, if it was an 'A' or 'B' side and finally if it was issued with a company or picture sleeve.

So if you're looking for a single with a particular title that you want, just turn to that page to see what is available.

I am a 'pure' Beatle fan / record collector and when I say 'pure', I mean John, Paul, George and Ringo, so if a single was produced when all four were a group, that is what I collect. However, there are some collectors that specialise in collecting earlier singles such as those recorded in Germany, circa 1961, on the Polydor label with Tony Sheridan and also the now-infamous Decca audition songs with Pete Best on drums. I have included these singles within this book for those specialist collectors of Beatle history.

I have not included in this edition any special singles such as picture discs, 10" singles and any re-releases after 1970 unless they have something of significance to the collector, i.e. re-issued in picture sleeve cover etc., I have avoided anything to do with the rarity or value.

Suffice it to say, 'If you want it and think it's worth it, buy it.'

1. <u>78 RPM Records</u>

78 RPM Records were produced for the less-affluent countries of the world, namely India, The Philippines, Colombia and Argentina. The same title compilations were also produced and issued on 45s; both 45s and 78s were generally issued at the same time.

Whilst 78 RPM Records were being faded out of production from circa 1957 in favour of 45s by most recording companies, some countries still issued 78s until circa 1967.

The reason for this was quite simple but maybe a little hard to comprehend for our younger generations. Not all countries had a comprehensive electrical power grid system at that period in time, so a record player that ran off electricity was of no use in those parts of these countries that had no access to this power grid. Therefore, they used old 'Clockwork Gramophone Machines' that had to be wound up by hand and that could only play 78 RPM Records. Nevertheless, records were still in demand, hence the production and issue of these records.

India and The Philippines were the main producers of 78s, all of which were issued in a company sleeve. Argentina only produced one 78 RPM which was issued in a picture sleeve (very sought after) Colombia-issued only two which also had company sleeves.

In this section of 78 RPM Records, you will find there are 84 different song titles and 54 different compilations (i.e. 54 collectable 78s).

78 RPM Singles
Titles

A Hard Day's Night

A Hard Day's Night / I Should Have Known Better

| Colombia | ODEON | NCO-300938 | 1964 | Company | 'B' Side |

A Hard Day's Night / Things We Said Today

| India | Parlophone | R.5160 | 1964 | Company | 'A' Side |
| Philippines | Parlophone | PAL 60197 | 1964 | Company | 'A' Side |

Act Naturally

Act Naturally / Yesterday

| India | Parlophone | DPE.184 | 1965 | Company | 'B' Side |

Act Naturally / It's Only Love

| Philippines | Parlophone | PAL60394 | 1965 | Company | 'A' Side |

All My Loving

All My Loving / Don't Bother Me

| Philippines | Parlophone | PAL60104 | 1963 | Company | 'A' Side |

And I Love Her

And I Love Her / If I Fell

| India | Parlophone | DPE.167 | 1964 | Company | 'B' Side |

And I Love Her / I Should Have Known Better

| Philippines | Parlophone | PAL 60218 | 1964 | Company | 'B' Side |

Anna

Anna / Misery

| Philippines | Parlophone | PAL 60272 | 1964 | Company | 'B' Side |

Any Time at All

Any Time at All / Tell Me Why

| Philippines | Parlophone | PAL 60219 | 1964 | Company | 'A' Side |

Ask Me Why

Ask Me Why / Please, Please Me

| India | Parlophone | R.4983 | 1963 | Company | 'B' Side |

Ask Me Why / There's a Place

| Philippines | Parlophone | PAL 60274 | 1964 | Company | 'A' Side |

Boys

Boys / I Saw Her Standing There

| Philippines | Parlophone | PAL 60101 | 1963 | Company | 'B' Side |

Can't Buy Me Love

Can't Buy Me Love / You Can't Do That

India	Parlophone	R.5014	1964	Company	'A' Side
Philippines	Parlophone	PAL 60161	1963	Company	'A' Side

Chains

Chains / PS I Love You

Philippines	Parlophone	PAL 60273	1964	Company	'B' Side

Day Tripper

Day Tripper / We Can Work It Out

India	Parlophone	R.5389	1965	Company	'B' Side

Devil in Her Heart

Devil in Her Heart /
Roll Over Beethoven

Philippines	Parlophone	PAL 60105	1963	Company	'B' Side

Dizzy Miss Lizzy

Dizzy Miss Lizzy / The Night Before

India	Parlophone	DPE.183	1965	Company	'A' Side

Do You Want to Know a Secret

Do You Want to Know a Secret /
Twist and Shout

Philippines	Parlophone	PAL 60103	1963	Company	'B' Side

Don't Bother Me

Don't Bother Me / All My Loving

| Philippines | Parlophone | PAL 60104 | 1963 | Company | 'B' Side |

Don't Bother Me

Don't Bother Me / I Saw Her Standing There

| Colombia | Odeon | NCO300855 | 1964 | Company | 'B' Side |

Drive My Car

Drive My Car / Norwegian Wood

| India | Parlophone | DPE.186 | 1965 | Company | 'B' Side |

Eight Days a Week

Eight Days a Week /
Every Little Thing

| Philippines | Parlophone | PAL 60282 | 1964 | Company | 'A' Side |

Eight Days A Week / I'm a Loser

| India | Parlophone | DPE.178 | 1965 | Company | B' Side |

Every Little Thing

Every Little Thing /
Eight Days a Week

| Philippines | Parlophone | PAL 60282 | 1964 | Company | 'B' Side |

From Me to You

From Me to You / I Saw Her Standing There

| Philippines | Parlophone | EGX 8883 | 1963 | Company | 'A' Side |

From Me to You / Thank You Girl

| India | Parlophone | R.5015 | 1963 | Company | 'A' Side |
| Philippines | Parlophone | PAL60107 | 1963 | Company | 'A' Side |

Good Day Sunshine

Good Day Sunshine / Here, There and Everywhere

| India | Parlophone | DPE.190 | 1966 | Company | 'B' Side |

Girl

Girl / Nowhere Man

| India | Parlophone | DPE.188 | 1966 | Company | 'B' Side |

Hello, Goodbye

Hello, Goodbye / I Am the Walrus

India	Parlophone	R.5655	1967		Company		'A' Side

Help

Help / I'm Down

India	Parlophone	R.5305	1965		Company		A' Side

Here, There and Everywhere

Here, There and Everywhere / Good Day Sunshine

India	Parlophone	DPE.190	1966		Company		'A' Side

Hey Jude

Hey Jude / Revolution

| India | Parlophone | DP 570 | 1965 | Company | 'A' Side |

Hold Me Tight

Hold Me Tight / Not a Second Time

| Philippines | Parlophone | PAL60269 | 1964 | Company | 'B' Side |

Honey Don't

Honey Don't / I'll Follow the Sun

Philippines	Parlophone	PAL60287	1964	Company	'A' Side

I Am the Walrus

I Am the Walrus /
Hello, Goodbye of Love

India	Parlophone	R 5655	1967	Company	'B' Side

I Call Your Name

I Call Your Name / Long Tall Sally

India	Parlophone	DP 164	1963	Company	'B' Side

I Don't Want to Spoil the Party

I Don't Want to Spoil the Party /
Words of Love

Philippines	Parlophone	PAL 60338	1965	Company	'A' Side

I Feel Fine

I Feel Fine / She's a Woman

India   Parlophone   R.5200   1964   Company   'A' Side

I Saw Her Standing There

I Saw Her Standing There / Boys

Philippines   Parlophone   PAL60101   1963   Company   'A' Side

I Saw Her Standing There / Don't Bother Me

Colombia   Odeon   NCO300855   1964   Company   'A' Side

I Saw Her Standing There / From Me to You

Philippines   Parlophone   EGX 8883   1963   Company   'B' Side

I Saw Her Standing There / Hold Me Tight

India   Parlophone   DPE.159   1963   Company   'A' Side

I Saw Her Standing There / Twist and Shout

Argentina   Odeon   POPS 75202   1964   Picture   'B' Side

I Should Have Known Better

I Should Have Known Better / A Hard Day's Night

Colombia	Odeon	NCO300938	1964	Company	'A' Side

I Should Have Known Better / And I Love Her

Philippines	Parlophone	PAL60218	1964	Company	'A' Side

I Should Have Known Better / I'm Happy Just to Dance

India	Parlophone	DPE.168	1964	Company	'B' Side

I Want to Be Your Man

I Want to Be Your Man / Till There Was You

Philippines	Parlophone	PAL60270	1964	Company	'A' Side

I Want to Hold Your Hand

I Want to Hold Your Hand / Please, Please Me

| Philippines | Parlophone | PAL 60102 | 1963 | Company | 'A' Side |

I Want to Hold Your Hand /
This Boy

| India | Parlophone | R.5084 | 1963 | Company | 'A' Side |
| Philippines | Parlophone | ? | ? | Company | 'A' Side |

If I Fell

If I Fell / And I Love Her

India	Parlophone	DPE.167	1964	Company	'A' Side

If I Fell / I'm Happy Just to Dance

Philippines	Parlophone	PAL 60217	1964	Company	'B' Side

I'll Cry Instead

I'll Cry Instead / Tell Me Why

India	Parlophone	DPE.172	1965	Company	'B' Side

I'll Follow the Sun

I'll Follow the Sun / Honey Don't

Philippines	Parlophone	PAL 60287	1964	Company	B' Side

I'll Follow the Sun / Words of Love

India	Parlophone	DPE.180	1965	Company	'A' Side

I'll Get You

I'll Get You / She Loves You

India	Parlophone	R.5055	1963	Company	'B' Side
Philippines	Parlophone	PAL 60106	1963	Company	'B' Side

I'm a Loser

I'm a Loser / Eight Days a Week

India	Parlophone	DPE.178	1965	Company	'A' Side

I'm a Loser / Mr. Moonlight

Philippines	Parlophone	PAL60284	1964	Company	'B' Side

I'm Down

I'm Down / Help

India	Parlophone	R.5305	1965	Company	'B' Side

I'm Happy Just to Dance

I'm Happy Just to Dance / If I Fell

| Philippines | Parlophone | PAL 60217 | 1964 | Company | 'A' Side |

I'm Happy Just to Dance /
I Should Have Known Better

| India | Parlophone | DPE.168 | 1964 | Company | 'A' Side |

It Won't Be Long

It Won't Be Long / Love Me Do

| Philippines | Parlophone | PAL 60263 | 1964 | Company | 'B' Side |

It's Only Love

It's Only Love / Act Naturally

Philippines	Parlophone	PAL60394	1965	Company	'B' Side

Long Tall Sally

Long Tall Sally / I Call Your Name

India	Parlophone	DPE.164	1963	Company	'A' Side

Lady Madonna

Lady Madonna / The Inner Light

India	Parlophone	R 5675	1968	Company	'A' Side

Love Me Do

Love Me Do / It Won't Be Long

Philippines	Parlophone	PAL 60263	1964	Company	'A' Side

Love Me Do / PS I Love You

India	Parlophone	R4949	1963	Company	'A' Side

Matchbox

Matchbox / Slow Down

Philippines	Parlophone	PAL60255	1964	Company	'B' Side

__Michelle__

Michelle / You Won't See Me

India	Parlophone	DPE.187	1966	Company	'A' Side

__Misery__

Misery / Anna

Philippines	Parlophone	PAL 60272	1964	Company	'A' Side

__Mr. Moonlight__

Mr. Moonlight / I'm a Loser

Philippines	Parlophone	PAL60284	1964	Company	'B' Side

No Reply

No Reply / Rock and Roll Music

India	Parlophone	DPE.179	1965	Company	'B' Side
Philippines	Parlophone	PAL60283	1964	Company	'A' Side

Nowhere Man

Nowhere Man / Girl

India	Parlophone	DPE.188	1966	Company	'A' Side

Norwegian Wood

Norwegian Wood / Drive My Car

India	Parlophone	DPE.186	1965	Company	'A' Side

Not a Second Time

Not a Second Time / Hold Me Tight

Philippines	Parlophone	PAL60269	1964	Company	'A' Side

OB-LA-DI OB-LA-DA

Ob-La-Di Ob-La-Da /
While My Guitar Gently Weeps

| India | Parlophone | DP 192 | 1966 | Company | 'A' Side |

PS I Love You

PS I Love You / Chains

| Philippines | Parlophone | PAL60273 | 1964 | Company | 'A' Side |

PS I Love You / Love Me Do

| India | Parlophone | R4949 | 1963 | Company | 'B' Side |

Please, Please Me

PLEASE, PLEASE ME / ASK ME WHY

| India | Parlophone | R.4983 | 1963 | Company | 'A' Side |

Please, Please Me / I Won't to Hold Your Hand

| Philippines | Parlophone | PAL 60102 | 1963 | Company | 'B' Side |

Please, Please Me

Please, Please Me /
Roll Over Beethoven

| Philippines | Parlophone | PAR 1206-1 | 1963 | Company | 'B' Side |

Revolution

Revolution / Hey Jude

| India | Parlophone | DP 570 | 1968 | Company | 'B' Side |

Rock and Roll Music

Rock and Roll Music / No Reply

| India | Parlophone | DPE.179 | 1965 | Company | 'A' Side |
| Philippines | Parlophone | PAL 60283 | 1964 | Company | 'B' Side |

Roll Over Beethoven

Roll Over Beethoven /
Devil in Her Heart

| Philippines | Parlophone | PAL 60105 | 1963 | Company | 'A' Side |

Roll Over Beethoven

Roll Over Beethoven /
Please, Please Me

| Philippines | Parlophone | PAL 1206-1 | 1963 | Company | 'A' Side |

She Loves You

She Loves You / I'll Get You

India	Parlophone	R.5055	1963	Company	'A' Side
Philippines	Parlophone	PAL 60106	1963	Company	'A' Side

She's a Woman

She's A Woman / I Feel Fine

India	Parlophone	R.5200	1964	Company	'B' Side

Slow Down

Slow Down / Matchbox

Philippines	Parlophone	PAL 60255	1964	Company	'A' Side

Tell Me What You See

Tell Me What You See / You Like Me Too Much

India   Parlophone   DPE 185   1965   Company   'B' Side

Tell Me Why

Tell Me Why / Any Time at All

Philippines   Parlophone   PAL60219   1964   Company   'B' Side

Tell Me Why / I'll Cry Instead

India   Parlophone   DPE.172   1965   Company   'A' Side

Thank You Girl

Thank You Girl / From Me to You

India	Parlophone	R.5015	1963	Company	'B' Side
Philippines	Parlophone	PAL 60107	1963	Company	'B' Side

The Inner Light

The Inner Light / Lady Madonna

India	Parlophone	R 5675	1968	Company	'B' Side

The Night Before

The Night Before / Dizzy Miss Lizzy

India	Parlophone	DPE.183	1965	Company	'B' Side

Things We Said Today

Things We Said Today /
A Hard Day's Night

India	Parlophone	R.5160	1964	Company	'B' Side
Philippines	Parlophone	PAL 60197	1964	Company	'B' Side

This Boy

This Boy / I Want to
Hold Your Hand

India	Parlophone	R.5084	1963	Company	'B' Side
Philippines	Parlophone	?	?	Company	'B' Side

Ticket to Ride

Ticket to Ride / Yes It Is

India	Parlophone	R.5265	1965	Company	'A' Side

Till There Was You

Till There Was You / I Want to Be Your Man

Philippines	Parlophone	PAL 60270	1964	Company	'B' Side

Twist and Shout

Twist and Shout /
Do You Want to Know a Secret

Philippines   Parlophone   PAL60103   1963   Company   A' Side

Twist and Shout / I Saw Her Standing There

Argentina   Odeon   POPS75202   1964   Picture   'A' Side

We Can Work It Out

We Can Work It Out / Day Tripper

India   Parlophone   R.5389   1965   Company   'A' Side

While My Guitar Gently Weeps

While My Guitar Gently Weeps /
Ob-La-Di, Ob-La-Da

India	Parlophone	DPE 182	1966	Company	'B' Side

Words of Love

Words of Love /
I Don't Want to Spoil the Party

Philippines	Parlophone	PAL60338	1965	Company	'B' Side

Words of Love / I'll Follow the Sun

India	Parlophone	DPE.180	1965	Company	'B' Side

Yes It Is

Yes It Is / Ticket to Ride

India	Parlophone	R.5265	1965	Company	'B' Side

Yesterday

Yesterday / Act Naturally

India	Parlophone	DPE.184	1965	Company	'A' Side

You Can't Do That

You Can't Do That / Can't Buy Me Love

India	Parlophone	R.5014	1964	Company	'B' Side
Philippines	Parlophone	PAL60161	1963	Company	'B' Side

You Like Me Too Much

You Like Me Too Much / Tell Me What You See

| India | Parlophone | DPE 185 | 1965 | Company | 'A' Side |

You Won't See Me

You Won't See Me / Michelle

| India | Parlophone | DPE.187 | 1966 | Company | 'B' Side |

2. 45 RPM Polydor Singles

As the 'Beatles' band wagon began to gather momentum in 1963, the Polydor label decided to cash in on the act, so they released the recordings that had been made previously with Tony Sheridan using the Beatles as his backing group, under the alias of 'The Beat Brothers'.

These records covered 14 different titles with 15 compilations from 19 different countries.

These were issued under license from Polydor, by six different record companies, namely, Amica, Atco, Decca, Konfektinsindustri, MGM and Polydor itself.

45 RPM Polydor Singles
Titles

Ain't She Sweet

Ain't She Sweet / Cry for a Shadow

E. Germany	Amiga	450 466	1965	Picture	'A' Side
Yugoslavia	Polydor	1220055	1981	Picture	'A' Side

Ain't She Sweet / If You Love Me Baby

W Germany	Polydor	52 317	1964	Picture	'A' Side
Chile	Polydor	52 317	1964	Company	'A' Side
Italy	Polydor	NH 52 317	1964	Picture	'A' Side
Japan	Polydor	DP-1369	1964	Picture	'A' Side
Peru	Polydor	L 70037F	1963	Company	'A' Side
Sweden	Polydor	52 317	1964	Picture	'A' Side
U K	Polydor	NH 52 317	1964	Company	'A' Side

Ain't She Sweet / Lucky Stuff

Sweden	Konfektion sindustri	Stuff 1	1964	Picture	'B' Side

Ain't She Sweet / Nobody's Child

Canada	Atco	6308	1964	Company	'A' Side
USA	Atco	6308	1964	Picture	'A' Side

Ain't She Sweet / Sam the Sham

Austria	Polydor	863 186-7	1964	Company	'A' Side

Ain't She Sweet / Sweet Georgia Brown

Mexico	Polydor	45-0380	1964	Company	'A' Side
Rhodesia	Polydor	PD7-8862	1964	Company	'A' Side
S Africa	Polydor	PD-8862	1964	Company	'A' Side

Ain't She Sweet / Take out Some Insurance on Me

W Germany	Polydor	52 317	1964	Picture	'A' Side
Australia	Polydor	NH 52 317	1964	Company	'A' Side
New Zealand	Polydor	NH 52 317	1964	Company	'A' Side

Cry for a Shadow

Cry for a Shadow / Ain't She Sweet

E. Germany	Amiga	450 466	1965	Picture	'B' Side
Yugoslavia	Polydor	1220055	1981	Picture	'B' Side

Cry for a Shadow / My Bonnie

Sweden	Polydor	NH10973	1964	Picture	'B' Side

Cry for a Shadow / Why

Australia	Polydor	NH 52 275	1964	Company	'A' Side
Canada	MGM	13227x	1964	Company	'B' Side
Chile	Polydor	69060	1964	Company	'A' Side
France	Polydor	52 275	1964	Company	'A' Side
W Germany	Polydor	52 275	1964	Picture	'B' Side
Japan	Polydor	DP 1362	1964	Picture	'B' Side
NewZealand	Polydor	NH 52 275	1964	Company	'A' Side
S Africa	Polydor	Jul/7 Pd 8819	1964	Company	'A' Side
UK	Polydor	NH 52 275	1964	Company	'A' Side
USA	MGM	K13227	1964	Picture	'B' Side

If You Love Me Baby

If You Love Me Baby /
Ain't She Sweet

W Germany	Polydor	52 317	1964	Picture	'B' Side
Chile	Polydor	52 317	1964	Company	'B' Side
Italy	Polydor	NH 52 317	1964	Picture	'B' Side
Japan	Polydor	DP-1369	1964	Picture	'B' Side
Peru	Polydor	L 70037F	1963	Company	'B' Side
Sweden	Polydor	52 317	1964	Picture	'B' Side
UK	Polydor	NH 52 317	1964	Company	'B' Side

Kansas City

Kansas City / What'd I Say

Japan	Polydor	DP-1429	1965	Picture	'B' Side
Japan	Polydor	DP-1429	1986	Picture	'B' Side

Lucky Stuff

Lucky Stuff / Ain't She Sweet

Sweden	Konfektionsindustri	Stuff 1	1964	Picture	'A' Side

My Bonnie

My Bonnie / Cry for A Shadow

Sweden	Polydor	NH 10973	1964	Picture	'A' Side

My Bonnie / Skinny Minny

WGermany	Polydor	2135 501	1968	Company	'B' Side

My Bonnie / The Saints

Australia	Polydor	NH 24-673	1963	Company	'A' Side
Belgium	Polydor	NH 52 273	1964	Picture	'A' Side
Canada	Decca	31382	1962	Company	'A' Side
Canada	MGM	13213x	1964	Company	'A' Side
Chile	Polydor	64055	1964	Company	'A' Side
France	Polydor	52 273	1964	Company	'A' Side
W Germany	Polydor	NH 24-673	1961	C & P	'A' Side
W Germany	Polydor	NH 24-673	1962	Picture	'A' Side
W Germany	Polydor	52 273	1964	Picture	'A' Side
Japan	Polydor	DP-1254	1962	Picture	'A' Side

Japan	Polydor	DP-1351	1964	Picture	'A' Side
Mexico	Polydor	45-0341	1964	Company	'A' Side
New Zealand	Polydor	NH 52 673	1964	Company	'A' Side
Peru	Polydor	L 70027F	1963	Company	'A' Side
S Africa	Polydor	Jul/7 Pd 8818	1963	Company	'A' Side
UK	Polydor	NH 66-833	1962	Company	'A' Side
UK	Polydor	NH 52 273	1964	Company	'A' Side
USA	Decca	31382	1962	Company	'A' Side
USA	MGM	K13213	1964	Picture	'A' Side

Nobody's Child

Nobody's Child / Ain't She Sweet

| Canada | Atco | 6308 | 1964 | Company | 'B' Side |
| USA | Atco | 6308 | 1964 | Picture | 'B' Side |

Nobody's Child / Sweet Georgia Brown

| W Germany | Polydor | 52 906 | 1964 | Company | 'B' Side |

Sam the Sham: Wooly Bully

Sam the Sham: Wooly Bully / Ain't She Sweet

| Austria | Polydor | 863 186-7 | 1964 | Company | 'B' Side |

Skinny Minny

Skinny Minny / My Bonnie

W Germany	Polydor	2135 501	1968	Company	'A' Side

Skinny Minny / Sweet Georgia Brown

W Germany	Polydor	52 324	1964	Company	'B' Side

Sweet Georgia Brown

Sweet Georgia Brown /
Ain't She Sweet

Mexico	Polydor	45-0380	1964	Company	'B' Side
Rhodesia	Polydor	PD7-8862	1964	Company	'B' Side
S Africa	Polydor	PD-8862	1964	Company	'B' Side

Sweet Georgia Brown /
Nobody's Child

UK	Polydor	NH 52 906	1964	Company	'A' Side

Sweet Georgia Brown /
Skinny Minny

W Germany	Polydor	52 324	1964	Company	'A' Side

Sweet Georgia Brown /
Take out Some Insurance on Me

USA	Atco	6302	1964	Company	'A' Side

Sweet Georgia Brown / Why

E Germany	Amiga	450 471	1965	Picture	'A' Side

Sweet Georgia Brown / Ya Ya

Greece	Polydor	66849	1963	Company	'B' Side

Take out Some Insurance on Me

Take out Some Insurance on Me / Ain't She Sweet

W Germany	Polydor	52 317	1964	Picture	'B' Side
Australia	Polydor	NH 52 317	1964	Company	'B' Side
New Zealand	Polydor	NH 52 317	1964	Company	'B' Side

Take out Some Insurance on Me / Sweet Georgia Brown

| USA | Atco | 6302 | 1964 | Company | 'B' Side |

The Saints

The Saints / My Bonnie

Australia	Polydor	NH 24-673	1963	Company	'B' Side
Belgium	Polydor	NH 52 273	1964	Picture	'B' Side
Canada	Decca	31382	1962	Company	'B' Side
Canada	MGM	13213x	1964	Company	'B' Side
Chile	Polydor	64055	1964	Company	'B' Side
France	Polydor	52 273	1964	Company	'B' Side
W Germany	Polydor	NH 24-673	1961	C.& P	'B' Side
W Germany	Polydor	NH 24-673	1962	Picture	'B' Side
W Germany	Polydor	52 273	1964	Picture	'B' Side
Japan	Polydor	DP-1254	1962	Picture	'B' Side
Japan	Polydor	DP-1351	1964	Picture	'B' Side
Mexico	Polydor	45-0341	1964	Company	'B' Side
New Zealand	Polydor	NH 52 673	1964	Company	'B' Side
Peru	Polydor	L 70027F	1963	Company	'B' Side
S Africa	Polydor	Jul/7 Pd 8818	1963	Company	'B' Side
UK	Polydor	NH 66-833	1962	Company	'B' Side
UK	Polydor	NH 52 273	1964	Company	'B' Side
USA	Decca	31382	1962	Company	'B' Side
USA	MGM	K13213	1964	Picture	'B' Side

What'd I Say

What'd I Say / Kansas City

Japan	Polydor	DP-1429	1965	Picture	'A' Side
Japan	Polydor	DP-1429	1986	Picture	'A' Side

Why

Why / Cry for a Shadow

Australia	Polydor	NH 52 275	1964	Company	'B' Side
Canada	MGM	13227x	1964	Company	'A' Side
Chile	Polydor	69060	1964	Company	'B' Side
France	Polydor	52 275	1964	Company	'B' Side
W Germany	Polydor	52 275	1964	Picture	'A' Side
Japan	Polydor	DP 1362	1964	Picture	'A' Side
New Zealand	Polydor	NH 52 275	1964	Company	'B' Side
S Africa	Polydor	Jul/7 Pd 8819	1964	Company	'B' Side
UK	Polydor	NH 52 275	1964	Company	'B' Side
USA	MGM	K13227	1964	Picture	'A' Side

Why / Sweet Georgia Brown

E Germany	Amiga	450 471	1965	Picture	'B' Side

Ya Ya

Ya Ya / Sweet Georgia Brown

Greece	Polydor	66849	1963	Company	'A' Side

3. 45 RPM Singles

45 RPM Singles are the most prolific of the Beatles' releases. They cover 163 titles with 247 different compilations from 45 countries. They were released on various record labels as listed below:

Apple	Jugoton	Parlophone
Amiga	Musart	Swan
Capitol	Odeon	Tollie
HMV	Oldies	Vee Jay
EMI	Bayly	Supraphon
Amiga		

I have not included anniversary/re-issues but have only listed original singles. I have, however, included in this section the Brazilian 45s issued on the EMI label around circa 1990 and the American 1994 'Juke Box' collection issued on the Capitol label, a full list of these records can be found further along in this book for easier reference to collectors.

45 RPM Singles

Titles

A Day in the Life

A Day in the Life / With a Little Help from My Friends / Sgt Pepper

Italy	Parlophone	PFC 7511	1967	Picture	'B' Side
Japan	Odeon	EAR-20501	1978	Picture	'B' Side
UK	Parlophone	R6022	1978	Picture	'B' Side
USA	Capitol	4612	1978	Company	'B' Side
USA	Capitol J/Box	S7-17701 (Crystal)	1994-96	Company	'B' Side

A Hard Day's Night

A Hard Day's Night / And I Love Her

Greece	Parlophone	GMSP 56	1964	Picture	'A' Side
Nicaragua	Apple	01-0515	1970	Picture	'B' Side

A Hard Day's Night / All My Loving

S Africa	Parlophone	SPD 331	1964	Company	'A' Side

A Hard Day's Night / I Should Have Known Better

Brazil	EMI	451 3398	19?	Picture	'A' Side
Canada	Capitol	5222	1964	Company	'A' Side
Canada	Capitol Target	5222	1969	Company	'A' Side
Chile	Odeon	MSOD 8464	1964	Company	'A' Side
Ecuador	Odeon	87430	1964	Company	'A' Side
France	Odeon	FOS 20.050	1967	Company	'A' Side
Peru	Odeon	9071	1964	Company	'B' Side
USA	Capitol	5222	1964	Picture	'A' Side
USA	Capitol Target	5222	1969	Company	'A' Side

A Hard Day's Night / Long Tall Sally

Bolivia	Odeon	BO 1055	1964	Picture	'A' Side
USA	Beat Records	2,1964	197?	Company	'A' Side

A Hard Day's Night /
Please Mr. Postman

Rhodesia	Parlophone	SPD 332	1964	Company	'B' Side
S Africa	Parlophone	SPD 332	1964	Company	'B' Side

A Hard Day's Night /
Roll Over Beethoven

Spain	Odeon	DSOL 66.057	1964	Company	'A' Side

A Hard Day's Night

A Hard Day's Night / Tell Me Why

France	Odeon	SO 10121	1964	Picture	'A' Side

A Hard Day's Night / Things We Said Today

Australia	Parlophone	A 8123	1964	Company	'A' Side
Austria	Parlophone	O 28521	1964	Picture	'A' Side
Belgium	Parlophone	R5160	1964	Company	'A' Side
Denmark	Parlophone	R5160	1964	Picture	'A' Side
Finland	Parlophone	DPY 668	1964	Company	'A' Side
W Germany	Odeon	22 760	1964	Company	'A' Side
Guatemala	Odeon	4261	?	Picture	'A' Side
India	Parlophone	45-R.5160	1964	Company	'A' Side
Ireland	Parlophone	R(I)5160	1964	Company	'A' Side
Israel	Parlophone	R5160	1964	Company	'A' Side
Italy	Parlophone	QSMP 16363	1964	Picture	'A' Side
Japan	Apple	AR-1119	1964	Picture	'A' Side
Japan	Odeon	OR-1119	1964	Picture	'A' Side
Japan	Odeon	EAR-20227	1977	Picture	'A' Side
Mexico	Musart	Musart 3669	1964	Company	'A' Side
Netherlands	Parlophone	R5160	1964	Picture	'A' Side
New Zealand	Parlophone	NZP 3167	1964	Company	'A' Side
Norway	Parlophone	R5160	1965	Picture	'A' Side
Philippines	Parlophone	PAL 60197	1964	Company	'A'Side
Sweden	Parlophone	R5160	1964	Picture	'A' Side
Turkey	Odeon	LA 5143	1964	Picture	'B' Side
UK	Parlophone	R5160	1964	Company	'A' Side
USA	CapitolJ/Box	S7-17692(White)	199496	Company	'A' Side

A Taste of Honey

A Taste of Honey / I'll Cry Instead

Netherlands	Parlophone	HHR 129	1964	Company	'B' Side
W Germany	Odeon	22 789	1964	Company	'B' Side

Across the Universe

Across the Universe / Two of Us

Philippines	Parlophone	PAL 60945	1970	Company	'A' Side
USA	Capitol J/Box	S7-18891(Crystal)	1994-96	Company	'A' Side

Act Naturally

Act Naturally / Another Girl

Turkey	Odeon	LA 4245	1965	Picture	'A' Side

Act Naturally / It's Only Love

Philippines	Parlophone	PAL 69394	1965	Company	'A' Side

Act Naturally / Yesterday

Australia	Parlophone	A 8173	1965	Company	'B' Side
Canada	Capitol	5498	1965	Comp & Pict	'B' Side
Canada	Capitol	5498	1969	Company	'B' Side
Chile	Odeon	MSOD 8545	1965	Company	'B' Side
Denmark	Odeon	DK 1635	1965	Picture	'B' Side
W Germany	Odeon	23 031	1965	Picture	'A' Side
India	Parlophone	45-DPE.184	1965	Company	'B' Side
Japan	Apple	AR-1437	1965	Picture	'A' Side
Japan	Odeon	OR-1437	1965	Picture	'A' Side
Japan	Apple	EAR-20030	1976	Picture	'A' Side

New Zealand	Parlophone	NZP 3192	1965	Company	'B' Side
Norway	Odeon	ND 7442	1965	Picture	'B' Side
Peru	Odeon	9415	1965	Company	'B' Side
Switzerland	Odeon	9 23 031	1965	Picture	'A' Side
USA	Capitol	5498	1965	Picture	'B' Side
USA	Capitol	Target 5498	1969	Company	'B' Side
USA	Capitol J/Box	S7-18901 (Pink)	1994-96	Company	'B' Side

All My Loving

All My Loving / A Hard Day's Night

S Africa	Parlophone	SPD 331	1964	Company	'B' Side

All My Loving / Can't Buy Me Love

Turkey	Odeon	LA 4144	1964	Picture	'A' Side

All My Loving / Don't Bother Me

Philippines	Parlophone	PAL 60104	1963	Company	'A' Side

All My Loving / Hold Me Tight

French	Odeon	MO 20005	1966	Picture	'B' Side

All My Loving / If I Fell

Greece	Parlophone	GMPS 63	1964	Picture	'A' Side

All My Loving / I Saw Her Standing There

Chile	Odeon	MSOD 8498	1964	Picture	'B' Side
Finland	Parlophone	DPY 659	1964	Company	'A' Side
Norway	Parlophone	SD 5958	1964	Picture	'A' Side
Sweden	Odeon	SD 5958	1964	Picture	'A' Side

All My Loving /
I Wanna Be Your Man

| W Germany | Odeon | 22 681 | 1964 | Company | 'A' Side |
| Netherlands | Odeon | O 29504 | 1964 | Company | 'A' Side |

All My Loving / It Won't Be Long

| French | Odeon | SO 10100 | 1963 | Picture | 'A' Side |

All My Loving / Love Me Do

Japan	Apple	AR-1094	1964	Picture	'A' Side
Japan	Odeon	OR-1094	1964	Picture	'A' Side
Japan	Apple	EAR-20244	1977	Picture	'A' Side
Rhodesia	Parlophone	SPD 313	1964	Company	'A' Side
S Africa	Parlophone	SPD 313	1964	Company	'A' Side

All My Loving / Roll Over Beethoven

| New Zealand | Parlophone | NZP 3158 | 1964 | Company | 'B' Side |
| Mexico | Musart | 3611 | 1964 | Company | 'B' Side |

All My Loving / Thank You Girl

| Italy | Parlophone | QMSP 16364 | 1964 | Picture | 'B' Side |

All My Loving / This Boy

| Canada | Capitol | 72144 | 1964 | Company | 'A' Side |
| Canada | Capitol | 72144 | 1969-70 | Company | 'A' Side |

All Together Now

All Together Now / Hey Bulldog

French	Apple	006-04982	1972	Picture	'A' Side
French	Apple	2c-10 04462	1976	Company	'A' Side
W Germany	Apple	2c-10 04462	1969	Picture	'A' Side
Italy	Parlophone	006-04462	1976	Company	'A' Side
Sweden	Apple	006-04982	1972	Picture	'A' Side

All You Need Is Love

All You Need Is Love / Baby You're a Rich Man

Australia	Parlophone	A8263	1967	Company	'A' Side
Austria	Odeon	0 23 560	1967	Picture	'A' Side
Belgium	Parlophone	R5620	1967	Picture	'A' Side
Brazil	EMI	45BT 94	19?	Picture	'A' Side
Canada	Capitol	5964	1967	Comp.&Pic	'A' Side
Canada	Capitol	5964	1969	Company	'A' Side
Chile	Odeon	MSOD8683	1967	Company	'A' Side
Denmark	Parlophone	R5620	1967	Picture	'A' Side
France	Odeon	FOS 103	1967	Comp.&Pic	'A' Side
Finland	Parlophone	R5620	1967	Company	'A' Side
Greece	Parlophone	GMSP 116	1967	Company	'A' Side
WGermany	Odeon	23 560	1967	Picture	'A' Side
India	Parlophone	45-R.5620	1967	Company	'A' Side
Ireland	Parlophone	R (I)5620	1967	Company	'A' Side
Italy	Parlophone	QMSP16408	1967	Picture	'A' Side
Japan	Apple	AR-1763	1967	Picture	'A' Side
Japan	Odeon	OR-1763	1967	Picture	'A' Side
Japan	Odeon	EAR-20235	1977	Picture	'A' Side
Lebanon	Parlophone	MOL 19	1967	Company	'A' Side
Mexico	Capitol	6226	1967	Picture	'A' Side
Netherlads	Parlophone	R5620	1967	Picture	'A' Side
NewZealand	Parlophone	NZP 3236	1967	Company	'A' Side
Nicaragua	Odeon	01-0151	1967	Company	'A' Side
Nigeria	Parlophone	45-R.5620	1967	Company	'A' Side
Norway	Parlophone	R5620	1967	Picture	'A' Side
Peru	Odeon	10004	1967	Company	'A' Side

Philippines	Parlophone	PAL 60673	1967	Company	'A' Side
Portugal	Parlophone	PDP 5082	1967	Company	'A' Side
Rhodesia	Parlophone	SPD 431	1967	Company	'A' Side
Singapore	Parlophone	R5620	1967	Company	'A' Side
S Africa	Parlophone	SPD 431	1967	Company	'A' Side
Spain	Odeon	DSOL 66.080	1967	Picture	'A' Side
Spain	Odeon	1J006-04476	1970	Picture	'A' Side
Sweden	Parlophone	R5620	1967	Picture	'A' Side
Turkey	Odeon	LA 4280	1967	Company	'A' Side
UK	Parlophone	R5620	1967	Company	'A' Side
USA	Capitol	5964	1967	Picture	'A' Side
USA	Capitol	Target 5964	1969	Company	'A' Side
USA	CapitolJ/Box	S7-17693(Pink)	1994-96	Company	'A' Side
W Indies	Parlophone	R5620	1967	Company	'A' Side
Yugoslavia	Parlophone/Jugoton	SP 8137	1967	Picture	'A' Side

And I Love Her

And I Love Her / A Hard Day's Night

Greece	Parlophone	GMSP 56	1964	Company	'B' Side
Nicaragua	Apple	01-0515	1970	Picture	'B' Side

And I Love Her / Any Time at All

Peru	Odeon	9098	1964	Company	'A' Side

And I Love Her / Can't Buy Me Love

Italy	Parlophone	PFC 7504	1966	Company	'B' Side

And I Love Her / Chains

Ecuador	Odeon	87518	1965	Company	'A' Side

And I Love Her / If I Fell

Canada	Capitol	Target 5235	1964	Company	'A' Side
Canada	Capitol	5235	1969-71	Company	'A' Side
Chile	Odeon	MSOD 8459	1964	Company	'A' Side
India	Parlophone	45-DPE.167	1964	Company	'B' Side
Italy	Parlophone	QMSP 16365	1964	Picture	'A' Side
Japan	Odeon	OR-1145	1964	Picture	'A' Side
Japan	Apple	AR-1145	1964	Picture	'A' Side
Japan	Odeon	EAR-20247	!	Picture	'A' Side
Netherlands	Parlophone	HHR 130	1964	Picture	'B' Side
USA	Capitol	5235	1964	Picture	'A' Side
USA	Capitol	Target 5235	1969	Company	'A' Side

And I Love Her / I'm Happy Just to Dance

Turkey	Odeon	LA 4158	1964	Picture	'B' Side

And I Love Her / I Should Have Known Better

Finland	Parlophone	DPY 672	1964	Company	'B' Side
W Germany	Odeon	22 792	1964	Company	'A' Side
Greece	Parlophone	GMSP 64	1964	Company	'B' Side
New Zealand	Parlophone	NZP 3172	1964	Company	'B' Side
Norway	Odeon	ND 743	1964	Picture	'B' Side
Philippines	Parlophone	PAL 60218	1964	Company	'B' Side

And I Love Her / Tell Me Why

Mexico	Musart	3761	1964	Company	'A' Side

Anna (Go to Him)

Anna (Go to Him) / Chains

Nigeria	Parlophone	45-DPN 304	1964	Company	'A' Side

Anna (Go to Him) / Dizzy Miss Lizzy

Japan	Apple	AR 1418	1965	Picture	'B' Side
Japan	Odeon	OR 1418	1965	Picture	'B' Side
Japan	Odeon	EAS-17062	1965	Picture	'B' Side

Anna (Go to Him) / Misery

Philippines	Parlophone	PAL 60272	1964	Company	'B' Side

Anna (Go to Him) / She's a Woman

Peru	Odeon	9157	1964	Company	'B' Side

Anna (Go to Him) / There's a Place

Chile	Odeon	MSOD 8533	1965	Picture	'B' Side

Another Girl

Another Girl / Act Naturally

Turkey	Odeon	LA 4245	1965	Picture	'B' Side

Another Girl / I Need You

Philippines	Parlophone	PAL 60395	1965	Company	'B' Side

Another Girl / The Night Before

Japan	Odeon	OR-1430	1965	Picture	'B' Side
Japan	Apple	AR-1430	1965	Picture	'B' Side
Japan	Odeon	EAS-17064	1980	Picture	'B' Side

Any Time at All

Any Time at All / And I Love Her

Peru	Odeon	9098	1964	Company	'B' Side

Any Time at All / I Should Have Known Better

Mexico	Musart	3721	1964	Company	'B' Side

Any Time at All / Tell Me Why

Philippines	Parlophone	PAL 60219	1964	Company	'A' Side

Ask Me Why

Ask Me Why / Anna (Go to Him)

| USA | Vee Jay | DJ No 8 | 1964 | Company | 'B' Side |

Ask Me Why / Misery

| W German | Odeon | 22 663 | 1964 | Company | 'B' Side |
| Netherlands | Odeon | O 29501 | 1963 | Company | 'A' Side |

Ask Me Why / Please, Please Me

Australia	Parlophone	A8080	1963	Company	'B' Side
Canada	Capitol	72090	1963	Company	'B' Side
Chile	Odeon	MSOD 8432	1963	Company	'B' Side
Denmark	Parlophone	R4983	1963	Picture	'B' Side
French	Odeon	SO 10087	1964	?	'B' Side
India	Parlophone	45-R.4983	1963	Company	'B' Side
Ireland	Parlophone	R(I)R4983	1963	Company	'B' Side
Italy	Parlophone	QMSP 16346	1963	Picture	'B' Side
Italy	Parlophone	SC006-04451	1970	Picture	'B' Side
Japan	Odeon	OR-1024	1964	Picture	'B' Side
Japan	Apple	AR-1024	1964	Picture	'B' Side
Japan	Odeon	EAR-20222	1977	Picture	'B' Side
New Zealand	Parlophone	NZP 3142	1963	Company	'B' Side
Nigeria	Parlophone	45-R4983 NI	1963	Company	'B' Side
Norway	Parlophone	R4983	1963	Picture	'B' Side
Pakistan	Parlophone	45-R.4983	1963	Company	'B' Side
Spain	Odeon	DSOL 66.041	1963	Company	'B' Side

Spain	Odeon	1J006-04451	1970	Picture	'B' Side
Sweden	Parlophone	R4983	1963	Company	'B' Side
S Africa	Parlophone	SPD 261	1963	Company	'B' Side
Turkey	Odeon	LA 4139	1963	Picture	'B' Side
UK	Parlophone	R4983	1963	Company	'B' Side
UK	Parlophone	R4983	1983	Company	'B' Side
USA	Vee Jay	VJ 498	1963	Company	'B' Side

Ask Me Why / There's a Place

| Philippines | Parlophone | PAL 60274 | 1964 | Company | 'B' Side |

Baby It's You

Baby It's You / Chains

Chile	Odeon	MSOD 8524	1965	Picture	'B' Side

Baby You're a Rich Man

Baby You're a Rich Man / All You Need Is Love

Australia	Parlophone	A8263	1967	Company	'B' Side
Austria	Odeon	0 23 560	1967	Picture	'B' Side
Belgium	Parlophone	R5620	1967	Picture	'B' Side
Canada	Capitol	5964	1967	Comp. & Picture	'B' Side
Canada	Capitol	5964	1969-70	Company	'B' Side
Chile	Odeon	MSOD8683	1967	Company	'B' Side
Denmark	Parlophone	R5620	1967	Picture	'B' Side
France	Odeon	FOS 103	1967	Comp. & Picture	'B' Side
Greece	Parlophone	GMSP 116	1967	Company	'B' Side
W Germany	Odeon	23 560	1967	Picture	'B' Side
India	Parlophone	45-R.5620	1967	Company	'B' Side
Ireland	Parlophone	R(I)5620	1967	Company	'B' Side
Italy	Parlophone	QMSP 16408	1967	Picture	'B' Side
Japan	Apple	AR-1763	1967	Picture	'B' Side
Japan	Odeon	OR-1763	1967	Picture	'B' Side
Japan	Odeon	EAR-20235	1977	Picture	'B' Side
Lebanon	Parlophone	MOL 19	1967	Company	'B' Side

Mexico	Capitol	6226	1967	Picture	'B' Side
Netherlands	Parlophone	R5620	1967	Picture	'B' Side
New Zealand	Parlophone	NZP 3236	1967	Company	'B' Side
Nicaragua	Odeon	01-0151	1967	Company	'B' Side
Nigeria	Parlophone	45-R.5620	1967	Company	'B' Side
Norway	Parlophone	R5620	1967	Picture	'B' Side
Peru	Odeon	10004	1967	Company	'B' Side
Philippines	Parlophone	PAL 60673	1967	Company	'B' Side
Portugal	Parlophone	PDP 5082	1967	Company	'B' Side
Rhodesia	Parlophone	SPD 431	1967	Company	'B' Side
Singapore	Parlophone	R5620	1967	Company	'B' Side
S Africa	Parlophone	SPD 431	1967	Company	'B' Side
Spain	Odeon	DSOL 66.080	1967	Picture	'B' Side
Spain	Odeon	1J006-04477	1970	Picture	'B' Side
Sweden	Parlophone	R5620	1967	Picture	'B' Side
Turkey	Odeon	LA 4280	1967	Company	'B' Side
UK	Parlophone	R5620	1967	Company	'B' Side
USA	Capitol	5964	1967	Picture	'B' Side
USA	Capitol	Target 5964	1969	Company	'B' Side
USA	Capitol J/Box	S7-17693 (Pink)	1967	Picture	'B' Side
W Indies	Parlophone	R5620	1967	Company	'B' Side
Yugoslavia	Parl/Jugoton	SP8137	1967	Picture	'B' Side

Baby's in Black

Baby's in Black / Eight Days a Week

Netherlands	Parlophone	HHR 135	1965	Picture	'B' Side

Baby's in Black / No Reply

Italy	Parlophone	QMSP 16370	1964	Picture	'B' Side

Baby's in Black / Real Love

UK	Apple	R6425	1996	Company	'B' Side
USA	Apple	NR7243 58544	1996	Picture	'B' Side

Baby's in Black / Rock and Roll Music

Mexico	Musart	3823	1965	Company	'B' Side

Back in the USSR

Back in the USSR /
Don't Pass Me By

Denmark	Apple	SD 6061	1969	Picture	'A' Side
Netherlands	Parlophone	SD 6061	1969	Picture	'A' Side
Norway	Parlophone	SD 6061	1969	Picture	'A' Side
Sweden	Apple	SD 6061	1969	Picture	'A' Side

Back in the USSR /
Ob-La-Di, Ob-La-Da

Italy	Apple	QMSP16447	1968	Comp&Picture	'B' Side

Back in the USSR /
Twist and Shout

Brazil	EMI	451 3402	19?	Picture	'A' Side
Chile	Odeon	1181	1974	Company	'A' Side
Guatemala	Odeon	4218	1976	Company	'A' Side
Philippines	Parlophone	PAL 61154	1971	Company	'A' Side
UK	Parlophone	R6016	1976	Picture	'A' Side

Because

Because / Oh Darling

Philippine	Parlophone	PAL 61152	1969	Company	'B' Side

Birthday

Birthday / Cry Baby Cry

Nicaragua	Odeon	O-0385	1969	Company	'A' Side

Birthday / Ob-La-De, Ob-La-Da

Peru	Apple	10570	1968	Company	'B' Side

Birthday / Taxman

USA	Capitol J/Box	S7-17488 (Green)	1994	Company	'A' Side
USA	Capitol J/Box	S7-17488 (Black)	1994	Company	'A' Side

Blackbird

Blackbird / While My Guitar Gently Weeps

USA	Capitol J/Box	S7-18892 (Blue)	1994-96	Company	'B' Side

Boys

Boys / I Saw Her Standing There

Philippines	Parlophone	PAL 60101	1963	Picture	'B' Side

Boys / Kansas City

Canada	Capitol	Starline 45-6066	1965	Company	'B' Side
USA	Capitol	Starline 6066	1965	Company	'A' Side
USA	Capitol	Target 5555	1969	Company	'B' Side

Boys / Love Me Do

France	Odeon	SO 10108	1963	Picture	'A' Side

Boys / Tell Me Why

Chile	Odeon	MSOD 8527	1965	Picture	'B' Side

Boys / Twist and Shout

Denmark	Parlophone	SD 5946	1963	Picture	'B' Side
Finland	Parlophone	DPY 654	1963	Company	'B' Side
W Germany	Odeon	22 581	1963	Company	'B' Side
New Zealand	Parlophone	NZP 3160	1964	Company	'B' Side
Norway	Parlophone	R5946	1963	Picture	'B' Side
Spain	Odeon	DSOL 66 055	1964	Picture	'B' Side
Sweden	Odeon	SD 5946	1963	Picture	'B' Side
UK	Parlophone	R6016	1976	Picture	'A' Side

Can't Buy Me Love

Can't Buy Me Love / All My Loving

Turkey	Odeon	LA 4144	1964	Picture	'B' Side

Can't Buy Me Love / And I Love Her

Italy	Parlophone	PFC 7504	1964	Company	'A' Side

Can't Buy Me Love / Misery

Chile	Odeon	MSOD8477	1964	Company	'A' Side

Can't Buy Me Love / Rock and Roll Music

Ecuador	Odeon	87514	1965	Company	'A' Side

Can't Buy Me Love / Thank You Girl

Greece	Parlophone	GMSP 47	1964	Company	'A' Side

Can't Buy Me Love / You Can't Do That

Australia	Parlophone	A8113	1964	Company	'A' Side
Austria	Parlophone	O 28518	1964	Picture	'A' Side
Belgium	Parlophone	R5114	1964	Company	'A' Side
Brazil	EMI	451 3400	19?	Picture	'A' Side
Canada	Capitol	5150	1964	Company	'A' Side

Canada	Capitol	Target 5150	1969-71	Company	'A' Side
Denmark	Parlophone	R5114	1964	Picture	'A' Side
France	Odeon	SO 10111	1964	Picture	'A' Side
Finland	Parlophone	DPY 662	1964	Company	'A' Side
W Germany	Odeon	22 697	1964	Company	'A' Side
India	Parlophone	45-R.5114	1964	Company	'A' Side
Ireland	Parlophone	R (I)5114	1964	Company	'A' Side
Italy	Parlophone	16361	1964	Picture	'B' Side
Japan	Apple	AR-1076	1964	Picture	'A' Side
Japan	Odeon	OR-1076	1964	Picture	'A' Side
Japan	Odeon	EAR-20225	1977	Picture	'A' Side
Mexico	Musart	3595	1964	Company	'A' Side
Netherlands	Parlophone	R5114	1964	Company	'A' Side
New Zealand	Parlophone	NZP 3157	1964	Company	'A' Side
Norway	Parlophone	R5114	1964	Picture	'A' Side
Pakistan	Parlophone	R5114	1964	Company	'A' Side
Peru	Odeon	8892	1964	Company	'A' Side
Philippines	Parlophone	PAL 60161	1963	Company	'A' Side
Rhodesia	Parlophone	SPD 304	1964	Company	'A' Side
S Africa	Parlophone	SPD 304	1964	Company	'A' Side
Sweden	Parlophone	R5114	1964	Picture	'A' Side
UK	Parlophone	R5114	1964	Company	'A' Side
USA	Capitol	5150	1964	Picture	'A' Side
USA	Capitol	Target 5150	1969	Company	'A' Side
USA	Capitol	S7-17690 (Green)	1964	Picture	'A' Side
W Indies	Capitol	5150	1965	Company	'A' Side

Chains

Chains / Anna

Nigeria	Parlophone	45-DPN 304	1964	Company	'B' Side

Chains / And I Love Her

Ecuador	Odeon	87518	1965	Company	'B' Side

Chains / Baby It's You

Chile	Odeon	MSOD 8524	1965	Picture	'A' Side

Chains / PS I Love You

Philippines	Parlophone	PAL 60273	1964	Company	'B' Side

Christmas Time Is Here Again

Christmas Time Is Here Again / Free as a Bird

UK	Apple	R6422		1995	Company	'B' Side
USA	Apple	NR7243-8 58497 7 0		1995	Company	'B' Side

Come Together

Come Together / Something

Australia	Apple	A8943	1969	Company	'B' Side
Brazil	EMI	45BT 101	19?	Picture	'B' Side
Canada	Apple	2654	1969	Company	'A' Side
Canada	Apple	2654	1969	Company	'B' Side
Chile	Apple	Apple 12	1969	Picture	'A' Side
Denmark	Apple	R5814	1969	Picture	'B' Side
Ecuador	Odeon	87862	1969	Company	'B' Side
France	Apple	2C006-04266	1969	Picture	'B' Side
Finland	Parlophone	R5814	1969	Company	'B' Side
Greece	Parlophone	GMSP 146	1969	Company	'B' Side
Guatemala	Odeon	4213	1976	Company	'B' Side
W Germany	Apple	1C006-04266	1969	Picture	'B' Side
India	Apple	45-R.5814	1969	Company	'B' Side
Ireland	Apple	R (I)5814	1969	Company	'B' Side
Israel	Apple	R5814	1969	Picture	'B' Side
Italy	Apple	QMSP 16461	1969	Picture	'B' Side
Italy	Apple	3C006-04266	1969	Picture	'B' Side
Japan	Apple	AR-2400	1969	Picture	'A' Side
Japan	Apple	EAR-20241	1977	Picture	'A' Side
Lebanon	Apple	R5814 / C006-04266MA	1969	Company	'B' Side
Mexico	Apple	6565	1969	Picture	'B' Side
Netherlands	Apple	5C006-04266	1969	Picture	'B' Side
New Zealand	Apple	NZP 3345	1969	Company	'B' Side
Norway	Apple	ND 7485	1969	Picture	'B' Side

Peru	Apple	10920	1969	Company	'A' Side
Philippines	Apple	PAL 60898	1969	Company	'A' Side
Portugal	Parlophone	8E006-04031	1969	Picture	'A' Side
Singapore	Apple	PEA-504	1969	Company	'B' Side
S Africa	Parlophone	SPD 520	1969	Company	'B' Side
Spain	Odeon	1J006-04266	1969	Picture	'B' Side
Sweden	Apple	R5814	1969	Picture	'B' Side
Turkey	Apple	LA 4313	1969	Company	'B' Side
UK	Apple	R5814	1969	Company	'B' Side
USA	Apple	2654	1969	Company	'B' Side
USA	Capitol J/Box	S7-17698 (Blue)	1994-96	Company	'B' Side
Venezuela	Odeon	OD-45-14	1969	Company	'A' Side
W Indies	Parlophone	S45-X-4699	1969	Company	'B' Side
Yugoslavia	Apple / Jugoton	SP 8334	1969	Picture	'B' Side

Come Together

Come Together / Oh Darling

Venezuela	Odeon	OD-45-153	1970	Company	'B' Side

Cry Baby Cry

Cry Baby Cry / Birthday

Nicaragua	Odeon	O-0385	1969	Company	'B' Side

Day Tripper

Day Tripper / We Can Work It Out

Australia	Parlophone	A8183	1965	Company	'B' Side
Belgium	Parlophone	R5389	1965	Picture	'B' Side
Brazil	Odeon	31c00604470	1970	Company	'A' Side
Brazil	EMI	45BT 89	19?	Picture	'A' Side
Canada	Capitol	5555	1965	Comp. & Picture	'A' Side
Canada	Capitol	Target 5555	1969-71	Company	'A' Side
Chile	Odeon	MSOD 8560	1965	Company	'B' Side
Denmark	Parlophone	R5389	1965	Picture	'B' Side
France	Odeon	SO 10133	1965	Picture	'B' Side
Finland	Parlophone	DPY 689	1965	Company	'B' Side
Greece	Parlophone	GMSP 101	1965	Company	'B' Side
W Germany	Odeon	23 122	1965	Picture	'B' Side
India	Parlophone	45-R.5389	1965	Company	'B' Side
Ireland	Parlophone	R (I)5389	1965	Company	'B' Side
Israel	Parlophone	R5389	1965	Company	'B' Side
Italy	Parlophone	QMSP 16388	1966	Picture	'B' Side
Italy	Apple	3C006-04108	1969	Picture	'B' Side
Japan	Apple	AR-1445	1966	Picture	'B' Side
Japan	Odeon	OR-1445	1966	Picture	'B' Side
Japan	Odeon	EAR-20231	1977	Picture	'B' Side
Mexico	Capitol	6025	1965	Comp. & Picture	'A' Side
Netherlands	Parlophone	R5389	1965	Picture	'B' Side

Country	Label	Number	Year	Sleeve	Side
New Zealand	Parlophone	NZP 3194	1965	Company	'B' Side
Nigeria	Parlophone	45-R-5389 NI	1965	Company	'B' Side
Norway	Parlophone	R5389	1965	Picture	'B' Side
Peru	Capitol	5555	1965	Company	'B' Side
Peru	Odeon	9448	1965	Company	'B' Side
Philippines	Parlophone	PAL 60436	1965	Company	'B' Side
Portugal	Parlophone	PDP 5081	1966	Company	'B' Side
Rhodesia	Parlophone	SPD 372	1965	Company	'B' Side
S Africa	Parlophone	SPD 372	1965	Company	'B' Side
Sweden	Parlophone	R5389	1965	Picture	'B' Side
Switzerland	Odeon	9 23 122	1965	Picture	'B' Side
Turkey	Odeon	LA 4246	1966	Picture	'B' Side
UK	Parlophone	R5389	1965	Company	'B' Side
USA	Capitol	5555	1965	Picture	'B' Side
USA	Capitol	Starline 5555	1969	Company	'B' Side
USA	Capitol	Target 5555	1969	Company	'B' Side
Venezuela	Odeon	70 MT 117	1965	Company	'B' Side

This record was issued as a double 'A' side, the letters 'A' and 'B' in this case only refer to which side was the most popular in that particular country.

Devil in Her Heart

Devil in Her Heart / From Me to You

Italy	Parlophone	QMSP 16355	1964	Picture	'B' Side

Devil in Her Heart / It Won't Be Long

E. Germany	Emiga	450493	1965	Picture	'B' Side

Devil in Her Heart / Roll Over Beethoven

Philippines	Parlophone	PAL60105	1963	Company	'B' Side

Dizzy Miss Lizzy

Dizzy Miss Lizzy / Anna

Japan	Odeon	OR-1418	1965	Picture	'A' Side
Japan	Apple	AR-1418	1965	Picture	'A' Side
Japan	Odeon	EAS-17062	1980	Picture	'A' Side

Dizzy Miss Lizzy / I Need You

Italy	Parlophone	QMSP 16385	1965	Picture	'B' Side
Italy	Parlophone	3C-006 04455	1965	Picture	'B' Side

Dizzy Miss Lizzy / The Night Before

India	Parlophone	45-DPE.183	1965	Company	'A' Side

Dizzy Miss Lizzy / Yesterday

Belgium	Parlophone	DP 563	1965	Picture	'B' Side
Congo	HMV	DP 563	1965	Company	'B' Side
Finland	Parlophone	DPY 686	1965	Company	'B' Side
Greece	Parlophone	GMSP 95	1965	Company	'B' Side
Mexico	Capitol	6020	1965	Company	'B' Side
Netherlands	Parlophone	HHR 138	1965	Picture	'A' Side
Sweden	Parlophone	SD 5983	1965	Picture	'A' Side
Turkey	Odeon	LA 4232	1965	Picture	'B' Side
UK	Parlophone	DP 563	1965	Company	'B' Side

Dizzy Miss Lizzy / Your Gonna Lose That Girl

Philippines	Parlophone	PAL 60396	1965	Company	'A' Side

Do You Want to Know a Secret

Do You Want to Know a Secret / Little Child

W Germany	Odeon	22 710	1964	Company	'A' Side

Do You Want to Know a Secret / Money

New Zealand	Parlophone	NZP 3163	1964	Company	'A' Side

Do You Want to Know a Secret / Roll Over Beethoven

Greece	Parlophone	GMSP 53	1964	Picture	'B' Side

Do You Want to Know a Secret / Thank You Girl

Canada	Capitol	72151	1964	Company	'B' Side
Italy	Bluebell	VJ VJ 587	1964	Picture	'B' Side
Japan	Odeon	OR-1093	1964	Picture	'A' Side
Japan	Apple	AR-1093	1964	Picture	'A' Side
Japan	Odeon	EAS-17055	?	Picture	'A' Side
USA	Vee Jay	VJ 587	1964	Picture	'B' Side
USA	Oldies	45-OL 149	1964	Company	'B' Side
USA	Capitol	Starline 6064	1965	Company	'B' Side

Do You Want to Know a Secret /
Twist and Shout

Chile	Odeon	MSOD 8454	1963	Company	'B' Side
Mexico	Musart	3615	1964	Company	'B' Side
Netherlands	Parlophone	HHR 125	1963	Company	'B' Side
Philippines	Parlophone	PAL 60103	1963	Company	'B' Side
Rhodesia	Parlophone	SPD 283	1963	Company	'B' Side
S Africa	Parlophone	SPD 283	1963	Company	'B' Side

Don't Bother Me

Don't Bother Me / All My Loving

| Philippines | Parlophone | PAL60104 | 1963 | Company | 'B' Side |

Don't Bother Me / I Saw Her Standing There

| France | Odeon | SO 10107 | 1963 | Picture | 'B' Side |

Don't Let Me Down

Don't Let Me Down / Get Back

Australia	Apple	A8763	1969	Company	'B' Side
Brazil	EMI	45BT 99	19?	Picture	'B' Side
Canada	Apple	2490	1969	Company	'B' Side
Chile	Apple	Apple 7	1969	Company	'B' Side
Denmark	Apple	R5777	1969	Picture	'B' Side
Ecuador	Odeon	87829	1969	Company	'B' Side
France	Apple	2C006-04084	1969	Picture	'B' Side
Greece	Parlophone	GMSP 139	1969	Company	'B' Side
W Germany	Apple	1C006-04084	1969	Picture	'B' Side
India	Apple	45-R.5777	1969	Company	'B' Side
Ireland	Apple	R (I)5777	1969	Company	'B' Side
Israel	Apple	R5777	1969	Picture	'B' Side
Italy	Apple	QMSP 16454	1969	Picture	'B' Side
Italy	Apple	3C006-04084	1969	Company	'B' Side
Japan	Apple	AR-2279	1969	Picture	'B' Side
Japan	Apple	EAR-20239	1977	Picture	'B' Side
Kenya	Parlophone	R5777	1969	Company	'B' Side
Lebanon	Apple	R5777	1969	Company	'B' Side
Lebanon	Parlophone	R5777	1969	Company	'B' Side
Malaysia	Apple	R5777	1969	Company	'B' Side
Mexico	Apple	6483	1969	Company	'B' Side
Mozambique	Bayal/Parlo-phone	1 5005	1969	Company	'A' Side
Netherlands	Apple	5C006-04084	1969	Picture	'B' Side
New Zealand	Apple	NZP 3325	1969	Company	'B' Side

Nicaragua	Odeon	O-0393	1969	Company	'B' Side
Nigeria	Apple	R5777	1969	Company	'B' Side
Norway	Parlophone	R5777	1969	Picture	'B' Side
Peru	Apple	10684	1969	Company	'B' Side
Philippines	Apple	PAL 60860	1969	Company	'B' Side
Portugal	Parlophone	PDP 5091	1969	Picture	'B' Side
Rhodesia	Parlophone	SPD 508	1969	Company	'B' Side
Singapore	Apple	R5777	1969	Company	'B' Side
S Africa	Parlophone	SPD 508	1969	Company	'B' Side
Spain	Odeon	1J006-04084	1969	Picture	'B' Side
Sweden	Apple	R5777	1969	Picture	'B' Side
Turkey	Apple	LA 4308	1969	Company	'B' Side
UK	Apple	R5777	1969	Company	'B' Side
USA	Apple	2531	1969	Company	'B' Side
Venezuela	Parlophone	7 PMT 536	1969	Company	'B' Side
W Indies	Parlophone	R5777	1969	Company	'B' Side
Yugoslavia	Apple / Jugoton	SAP 8279	1969	Company	'B' Side

Don't Pass Me By

Don't Pass Me By /
Back in the USSR

Denmark	Apple	SD 6061	1969	Picture	'B' Side
Netherlands	Parlophone	SD 6061	1969	Picture	'B' Side
Norway	Parlophone	SD 6061	1969	Picture	'B' Side
Sweden	Apple	SD 6061	1969	Picture	'B' Side

Drive My Car

Drive My Car / Girl

France	Odeon	FOS 104	1966	Company	'B' Side

Drive My Car / Michelle

Belgium	Parlophone	DP 564	1966	Company	'B' Side
Congo	Parlophone	DP 564	1966	Company	'B' Side
Nigeria	Parlophone	45-DP 564	1966	Company	'A' Side
Turkey	Odeon	LA 4252	1966	Picture	'B' Side
UK	Parlophone	DP 564	1966	Company	'B' Side

Drive My Car / Norwegian Wood

India	Parlophone	45-DPE.186	1965	Company	'B' Side

Drive My Car / Nowhere Man

S Africa	Parlophone	SPD 381	1966	Company	'B' Side

Drive My Car / You Won't See Me

Philippines	Parlophone	PAL 60470	1966	Company	'A' Side

Eight Days a Week

Eight Days a Week / Baby's in Black

Netherlands	Parlophone	HHR 135	1965	Picture	'A' Side

Eight Days a Week / Every Little Thing

Philippines	Parlophone	PAL 60282	1964	Picture	'A' Side

Eight Days a Week / I Don't Want to Spoil the Party

Bolivia	Parlophone	BO-1040	1965	Picture	'A' Side
Canada	Capitol	5371	1965	Comp.& Picture	'A' Side
Canada	Capitol	Target 5371	1969-71	Company	'A' Side
Greece	Parlophone	GMSP 82	1965	Picture	'A' Side
Mexico	Musart	3821	1965	Company	'A' Side
USA	Capitol	5371	1965	Picture	'A' Side
USA	Capitol	Target 5371	1969	Company	'A' Side
USA	Apple	5371	1971	Company	'A' Side

Eight Days a Week / I'll Follow the Sun

Chile	Odeon	MSOD 8510	1965	Company	'A' Side

Eight Days a Week / I'm a Loser

Italy	Parlophone	QMSP 16377	1965	Picture	'A' Side
India	Parlophone	45-DPE.178	1965	Company	'B' Side

Eight Days a Week / No Reply

Ecuador	Odeon	87496	1965	Company	'A' Side
W German	Odeon	22 893	1965	Picture	'B' Side
Japan	Apple	AR-1189	1965	Picture	'B' Side
Japan	Odeon	OR-1189	1965	Picture	'B' Side
Japan	Odeon	EAS-17058	1977	Picture	'B' Side
New Zealand	Parlophone	NZP 3179	1964	Company	'A' Side
Switzerland	Odeon	9 922 893	1965	Picture	'B' Side

Eight Days a Week / Rock and Roll Music

Brazil	EMI	451 3396	19?	Picture	'B' Side
Denmark	Odeon	ND 7438	1965	Picture	'B' Side
Finland	Parlophone	DPY 678	1965	Company	'B' Side
France	Odeon	SO 10128	1964	Picture	'A' Side
Norway.	Odeon	ND 7438	1965	Company	'B' Side
Turkey.	Odeon	LA 4196	1965	Picture	'A' Side
S Africa	Parlophone	SPD?	1965	Company	'A' Side

Eight Days a Week / Ticket to Ride

Peru	Odeon	9247	1965	Company	'B' Side

Eleanor Rigby

Eleanor Rigby / Yellow Submarine

Australia	Parlophone	A8713	1966	Company	'B' Side
Belgium	Parlophone	R5493	1966	Company	'B' Side
Brazil	EMI	45BT 92	19?	Company	'B' Side
Canada	Capitol	5715	1966	Comp. & Picture	'B' Side
Canada	Capitol	5715	1969-70	Company	'B' Side
Chile	Odeon	MSOD 8616	1966	Company	'B' Side
Denmark	Parlophone	R5493	1966	Picture	'B' Side
Finland	Parlophone	DPY 703	1966	Company	'B' Side
France	Odeon	FOS 110	1967	Company	'B' Side
Greece	Parlophone	GMSP 109	1966	Company	'B' Side
Guatemala	Odeon	4206	1976	Company	'B' Side
W Germany	Odeon	23 280	1976	Picture	'B' Side
India	Parlophone	45-R.5493	1966	Company	'A' Side
Ireland	Parlophone	R (I)5786	1966	Company	'B' Side
Italy	Parlophone	QMSP 16397	1966	Picture	'B' Side
Japan	Apple	AR-1578	1966	Picture	'B' Side
Japan	Odeon	OR-1578	1966	Picture	'B' Side
Japan	Apple	EAR-20233	1977	Picture	'B' Side
Mexico	Capitol	6087	1966	Comp. & Picture	'B' Side
Netherlands	Parlophone	R5493	1966	Picture	'B' Side
New Zealand	Parlophone	NZP 3212	1966	Company	'B' Side

Nicaragua	Capitol	C-1104 (18396)	1966	Company	'B' Side
Norway	Parlophone	R5493	1966	Picture	'B' Side
Peru	Odeon	9635	1966	Company	'B' Side
Philippines	Parlophone	PAL 60549	1967	Company	'A' Side
Rhodesia	Parlophone	SPD 393	1966	Company	'A' Side
S Africa	Parlophone	SPD 393	1966	Company	'A' Side
Sweden	Parlophone	R5493	1966	Picture	'B' Side
Switzerland	Odeon	9 23 280	1966	Picture	'B' Side
Turkey	Odeon	LA 4263	1966	Company	'B' Side
UK	Parlophone	R5493	1966	Company	'B' Side
USA	Capitol	5715	1966	Picture	'B' Side
USA	Capitol	Target 5715	1969	Company	'B' Side
USA	Capitol J/Box	S7-17696 (Yellow)	1994-96	Company	'B' Side

Every Little Thing

Every Little Thing / Eight Days a Week

Philippines	Parlophone	PAL60282	1964	Company	'B' Side

Every Little Thing / Rock and Roll Music

Japan	Odeon	OR-1192	1965	Picture	'B' Side
Japan	Apple	AR-1192	1965	Picture	'B' Side
Japan	Odeon	EAR-20249	1977	Picture	'B' Side

Everybody's Trying to Be My Baby

Everybody's Trying to Be My Baby / Honey Don't

Greece	Parlophone	GMSP 75	1964		Company	'A' Side

Everybody's Trying to Be My Baby / I Don't Want to Spoil the Party

Japan	Odeon	OR-1195	1965	Picture	'B' Side
Japan	Apple	AR-1195	1965	Picture	B' Side
Japan	Odeon	EAS-17061	?	Picture	'B' Side

Everybody's Trying to Be My Baby / What You're Doing

Greece	Parlophone	GMSP 83	1965	Picture	'A' Side
Philippines	Parlophone	PAL 60339	1965	Company	'B' Side

Fool on the Hill

Fool on the Hill /
Magical Mystery Tour

| USA | Capitol J/Box | S7-18890 (Yellow) | 1994-96 | Company | 'B' Side |

Free as a Bird

Free as a Bird / Christmas Tome Is Here Again

UK	Apple	R6422	1995	Picture	'A' Side
USA	Apple	NR 7243 8 58497 7 0	1995	Picture	'A' Side

From Me to You

From Me to You / Devil in Her Heart

Italy	Parlophone	QMSP 16355	1964	Picture	'A' Side

From Me to You / I Saw Her Standing There

Japan	Apple	AR-1077	1964	Picture	'A' Side
Japan	Apple	AR-1077	1964	Picture	'A' Side
Japan	Apple	EAS-17054	?	Picture	'A' Side
Philippines	Parlophone	EGX 8883	1963	Company	A' Side

From Me to You / Please, Please Me

Brazil	EMI	451 3392	19?	Picture	'A' Side
Canada	Capitol	Starline 6063	1965	Company	'A' Side
Greece	Parlophone	GMSP 41	1963	Company	'B' Side
Italy	Bluebell	VJ 581	1964	Picture	'B' Side
USA	Capitol	Starline 6063	1965	Company	'B' Side
USA	Vee Jay	VJ 581	1964	Picture	'B' Side
USA	oldies	45 OL 150	1964	Company	'B' Side

From Me to You /
PS I Love You

Sweden	Odeon	SD5944	1963	Picture	'A' Side

From Me to You / Thank You Girl

Australia	Parlophone	A 8083	1963	Company	'A' Side
Canada	Capitol	72101	1963	Company	'A' Side
Chile	Odeon	MSOD 8440	1963	Company	'A' Side
Denmark	Parlophone	R5015	1963	Picture	'A' Side
Finland	Parlophone	DPY 652	1963	Company	'A' Side
W Germany	Odeon	22 416	1963	Company	'A' Side
Ireland	Parlophone	R (I)5015	1963	Company	'A' Side
India	Parlophone	45-R.5051	1963	Company	'A' Side
Netherlands	Odeon	45-O-29470	1963	Company	'A' Side
New Zealand	Parlophone	NZP 3143	1963	Company	'A' Side
Norway	Parlophone	R5015	1963	Picture	'A' Side
Peru	Odeon	8977	1964	Company	'A' Side
Philippines	Parlophone	PAL 60107	1963	Company	'A' Side
Rhodesia	Parlophone	SPD 267	1963	Company	'A' Side
S Africa	Parlophone	SPD 267	1963	Company	'A' Side
Turkey	Odeon	LA 4137	1963	Picture	'A' Side
UK	Parlophone	R5015	1963	Company	'A' Side
USA	Vee Jay	VJ 522	1963	Company	'A' Side

From Me to You / This Boy

Mexico	Musart	3596	1964	Company	'A' Side

From Me to You

From Me to You / Devil in Her Heart

Italy	Parlophone	QMSP 16355	1964	Picture	'A' Side

From Me to You / I Saw Her Standing There

Japan	Apple	AR-1077	1964	Picture	'A' Side
Japan	Apple	AR-1077	1964	Picture	'A' Side
Japan	Apple	EAS-17054	?	Picture	'A' Side
Philippines	Parlophone	EGX 8883	1963	Company	'A' Side

From Me to You / Please, Please Me

Brazil	EMI	451 3392	19?	Picture	'A' Side
Canada	Capitol	Starline 6063	1965	Company	'B' Side
Greece	Parlophone	GMSP 41	1963	Company	'B' Side
Italy	Bluebell	VJ 581	1964	Picture	'B' Side
USA	Capitol	Starline 6063	1965	Company	'B' Side
USA	Vee Jay	VJ 581	1964	Picture	'B' Side
USA	oldies	45 OL 150	1964	Company	'B' Side

From Me to You / PS I Love You

Sweden	Odeon	SD 5944	1963	Picture	'A' Side

From Me to You / Thank You Girl

Australia	Parlophone	A 8083	1963	Company	'A' Side
Canada	Capitol	72101	1963	Company	'A' Side

Chile	Odeon	MSOD 8440	1963	Company	'A' Side
Denmark	Parlophone	R5015	1963	Picture	'A' Side
Finland	Parlophone	DPY 652	1963	Company	'A' Side
W Germany	Odeon	22 416	1963	Company	'A' Side
Ireland	Parlophone	R (I)5015	1963	Company	'A' Side
India	Parlophone	45-R.5051	1963	Company	'A' Side
Netherlands	Odeon	45-O-29470	1963	Company	'A' Side
New Zealand	Parlophone	NZP 3143	1963	Company	'A' Side
Norway	Parlophone	R5015	1963	Picture	'A' Side
Peru	Odeon	8977	1964	Company	'A' Side
Philippines	Parlophone	PAL 60107	1963	Company	'A' Side
Rhodesia	Parlophone	SPD 267	1963	Company	'A' Side
S Africa	Parlophone	SPD 267	1963	Company	'A' Side
Turkey	Odeon	LA 4137	1963	Picture	'A' Side
UK	Parlophone	R5015	1963	Company	'A' Side
USA	Vee Jay	VJ 522	1963	Company	'A' Side

From Me to You / This Boy

Mexico	Musart	3596	1964	Company	'A' Side

Get Back

Get Back / Don't Let Me Down

Australia	Apple	7XCE21296	1969	Company	'A' Side
Brazil	Apple	A8763	1969	Company	'A' Side
Brazil	EMI	45BT 99	19?	Picture	'A' Side
Canada	Apple	2490	1969	Company	'A' Side
Chile	Apple	Apple 7	1969	Company	'A' Side
Denmark	Apple	R5777	1969	Picture	'A' Side
Ecuador	Odeon	87829	1969	Company	'A' Side
France	Apple	2C006-04084	1969	Picture	'A' Side
Greece	Parlophone	GMSP 139	1969	Company	'A' Side
W Germany	Apple	1C006-04084	1969	Picture	'A' Side
India	Apple	45-R.5777	1969	Company	'A' Side
Ireland	Apple	R (I)5777	1969	Company	'A' Side
Israel	Apple	R5777	1969	Picture	'A' Side
Italy	Apple	QMSP 16454	1969	Picture	'A' Side
Italy	Apple	3C006-04084	1969	Company	'A' Side
Japan	Apple	AR-2279	1969	Picture	'A' Side
Japan	Apple	EAR-20239	1977	Picture	'A' Side
Kenya	Parlophone	R5777	1969	Company	'A' Side
Lebanon	Apple	R5777	1969	Company	'A' Side
Lebanon	Parlophone	R5777	1969	Company	'A' Side
Malaysia	Apple	R5777	1969	Company	'A' Side
Mexico	Apple	6483	1969	Company	'A' Side
Mozambique	Bayal/Parlophone	1 5005	1969	Company	'A' Side
Netherlands	Apple	5C006-04084	1969	Picture	'A' Side
New Zealand	Apple	NZP 3325	1969	Company	'A' Side

Nicaragua	Odeon	O-0393	1969	Company	'A' Side
Nigeria	Apple	R5777	1969	Company	'A' Side
Norway	Parlophone	R5777	1969	Picture	'A' Side
Peru	Apple	10684	1969	Company	'A' Side
Philippines	Apple	PAL 60860	1969	Company	'A' Side
Portugal	Parlophone	PDP 5091	1969	Picture	'A' Side
Rhodesia	Parlophone	SPD 508	1969	Company	'A' Side
Singapore	Apple	R5777	1969	Company	'A' Side
S Africa	Parlophone	SPD 508	1969	Company	'A' Side
Spain	Odeon	1J006-04084	1969	Picture	'A' Side
Sweden	Apple	R5777	1969	Picture	'A' Side
Turkey	Apple	LA 4308	1969	Company	'A' Side
UK	Apple	R5777	1969	Company	'A' Side
USA	Apple	2490	1969	Company	'A' Side
Venezuela	Parlophone	7 PMT 536	1969	Company	'A' Side
W Indies	Parlophone	R5777	1969	Company	'A' Side
Yugoslavia	Apple / Jugoton	SAP 8279	1969	Company	'A' Side

Get Back / Let It Be

Japan	Odeon	EAR-20501	1981	Picture	'A' Side

Girl

Girl / Drive My Car

French	Odeon	FOS 104	1967	Company	'A' Side

Girl / If I Needed Someone

Philippines	Parlophone	PAL 60527	1967	Company	'A' Side

Girl / Nowhere Man

French	Odeon	2C-10 04474	1976	Company	'A' Side
India	Parlophone	45-DPE 188	1966	Company	'A' Side
Italy	Parlophone	QMSP 16398	1966	Picture	'A' Side
Italy	Parlophone	PFC 7506	1966	Company	'B' Side

Girl / Michelle

Denmark	Odeon	SD 5987	1966	Picture	'B' Side
Ecuador	Odeon	87596	1966	Company	'A' Side
Finland	Parlophone	DPY 696	1966	Company	'B' Side
W Germany	Odeon	23 152	1966	Picture	'B' Side
Netherlands	Parlophone	HHR 139	1966	Picture	'B' Side
Norway	Parlophone	SD 5987	1966	Picture	'B' Side
Sweden	Parlophone	SD 5987	1966	Picture	'B' Side
Switzerland	Odeon	9 23 152	1966	Picture	'B' Side
Turkey	Odeon	LA 4252	1966	Picture	'B' Side
UK	Parlophone	DP 564	1966	Company	'B' Side
USA	Apple	2531	1969	Picture	'A' Side
Venezuela	Apple	AP1821`	1973	Company	'A' Side

Girl / Run for Your Life

Chile	Odeon	MSOD 8600	1966	Company	'A' Side

Girl / You're Gonna Lose That Girl

USA	Capitol	4506	1971	Picture	'A' Side

Good Day Sunshine

Good Day Sunshine / Got to Get You into My Life

Mexico	Capitol	EPRO-003	1966	Company	'B' Side

Good Day Sunshine / Here, There and Everywhere

India	Parlophone	45-DPE.190	1966	Company	'B' Side
USA	Capitol J/Box	S7-18897(Orange)	1994-96	Company	'B' Side

Got to Get You into My Life

Got to Get You into My Life / Helter Skelter

Australia	Parlophone	A-11182	?	Company	'B' Side
Guatemala	Odeon	4231	1976	Picture	'A' Side
Japan.	Odeon	EAR-20050	1976	Picture	'B' Side
Mexico	Capitol	EPRO-003	1966	Company	'A' Side

| USA | Capitol | 4274 | 1976 | Company | 'A' Side |
| USA | Capitol J/Box | S7-18899 (Orange) | 1994-96 | Company | 'A' Side |

Happiness Is a Warm Gun

Happiness Is a Warm Gun /
Od-La-Di, Ob-La-Da

Finland   Parlophone   DPY 990   1968   Company   'B' Side

Hello, Goodbye

Hello, Goodbye / I Am the Walrus

Australia	Parlophone	A8273	1967	Company	'A' Side
Belgium	Parlophone	R5655	1967	Picture	'A' Side
Brazil	EMI	45BT 95	19?	Picture	'A' Side
Canada	Capitol	2056	1967	Comp. & Pic	'A' Side
Canada	Capitol	Target 2056	1969-71	Company	'A' Side
Chile	Odeon	MSOD 8719	1967	Company	'A' Side
Congo	Parlophone	R5655	1967	Picture	'A' Side
Denmark	Parlophone	R5655	1967	Picture	'A' Side
France	Parlophone	R5655	1967	Company	'A' Side
France	Odeon	FOS 106	1967	Picture	'A' Side
Finland	Parlophone	R5655	1967	Picture	'A' Side
Greece	Parlophone	GMSP 122	1967	Company	'A' Side
WGermany	Odeon	23 660	1967	Picture	'A' Side
India	Parlophone	45-R.5655	1967	Company	'B' Side
Ireland	Parlophone	R (I)5655	1967	Company	'A' Side
Italy	Parlophone	QMSP 16415	1967	Picture	'A' Side
Japan	Apple	AR-1838	1968	Picture	'A' Side
Japan	Odeon	OR-1838	1968	Picture	'A' Side
Japan	Odeon	EAR-20236	1977	Picture	'A' Side
Kenya	Parlophone	R 5655	1967	Company	'A' Side
Lebanon	Parlophone	MOL 10	1967	Company	'A' Side
Mexico	Capitol	6275	1967	Picture	'A' Side
Netherlands	Parlophone	R5655	1967	Picture	'A' Side
NewZealand	Parlophone	NZP 3249	1967	Company	'A' Side
Nicaragua	Odeon	O-0206	1967	Company	'B' Side
Norway	Parlophone	R5655	1967	Picture	'A' Side

Peru	Odeon	10143	1967	Company	'A' Side
Philippines	Parlophone	PAL 60714	1967	Company	'A' Side
Portugal	Parlophone	PDP 5083	1967	Company	'A' Side
Rhodesia	Parlophone	SPD 442	1967	Company	'A' Side
Singapore	Parlophone	R5655	1967	Company	'A' Side
S Africa	Parlophone	SPD 442	1967	Comp. & Pic	'A' Side
Spain	Odeon	DSOL 66.082	1967	Picture	'A' Side
Spain	Odeon	1J006-04477	1970	Picture	'A' Side
Sweden	Parlophone	R5655	1967	Picture	'A' Side
Turkey	Odeon	LA 4284	1967	Comp. & Pic	'A' Side
UK	Parlophone	R5655	1967	Company	'A' Side
USA	Capitol	2056	1967	Picture	'A' Side
USA	Capitol	Target 2056	1969	Company	'A' Side

Help

Help / I'm Down

Australia	Parlophone	A8163	1965	Company	'A' Side
Belgium	Parlophone	R5305	1965	Picture	'A' Side
Brazil	EMI	451 3399	19?	Picture	'A' Side
Canada	Capitol	5476	1965	Comp. &Pic	'A' Side
Canada	Capitol	2056	1969	Company	'A' Side
Chile	Odeon	MSOD 8535	1965	Company	'A' Side
Congo	HMV	R5305	1965	Company	'A' Side
Denmark	Parlophone	R5305	1965	Picture	'A' Side
France	Odeon	SO 10130	1965	Picture	'A' Side
Finland	Parlophone	DPY 684	1965	Company	'A' Side
Greece	Parlophone	GMSP 79	1965	Company	'A' Side
Guatemala	Odeon	4256	1976	Picture	'A' Side
W Germany	Odeon	23 023	1965	Picture	'A' Side
India	Parlophone	45-R.5305	1965	Company	'A' Side
Ireland	Parlophone	R (I)5305	1965	Company	'A' Side
Italy	Parlophone	QMSP 16383	1965	Picture	'A' Side
Japan	Apple	AR-1412	1965	Picture	'A' Side
Japan	Odeon	OR-1412	1965	Picture	'A' Side
Japan	Odeon	EAR-20230	1977	Picture	'A' Side
Netherlands	Parlophone	R5305	1965	Picture	'A' Side
New Zealand	Parlophone	NZP 3187	1965	Company	'A' Side
Nigeria	Parlophone	45-R.5305	1965	Company	'A' Side
Norway	Parlophone	R5305	1965	Picture	'A' Side
Peru	Odeon	9329	1965	Company	'A' Side

Philippines	Parlophone	PAL 60376	1965	Company	'A' Side
Rhodesia	Parlophone	SPD 363	1965	Company	'A' Side
S Africa	Parlophone	SPD 363	1965	Company	'A' Side
Sweden	Parlophone	R5305	1965	Picture	'A' Side
Switzerland	Odeon	9 923 023	1965	Picture	'A' Side
Turkey	Odeon	LA 4221	1965	Picture	'A' Side
UK	Parlophone	R5305	1965	Company	'A' Side
USA	Capitol	5476	1965	Picture	'A' Side
USA	Capitol	Target 5476	1969	Company	'A' Side
USA	Capitol J/Box	S717691 (White)	1994-96	Company	'A' Side

Help / I Need You

Ecuador	Odeon	87545	1965	Company	'A' Side
Mexico	Capitol	6011	1965	Company	'A' Side

Help / Michelle

Nicaragua	Odeon	O-0360	1969	Company	'B' Side

Helter Skelter

Helter Skelter / Got to Get You into My Life

Australia.	Parlophone	A-11182	?	Company	'B' Side
Guatemala	Odeon	4231	1976	Picture	'A' Side
Japan	Odeon	EAR-20050	1976	Picture	'A' Side
USA	Capitol	4274	1976	Company	'B' Side
USA	Capitol J/Box	S7-18899 (Orange)	1994-96	Company	'B' Side

Helter Skelter / Honey Pie

Venezuela	Parlophone	7 PMT 534	1968	Company	'A'Side

Here Comes the Sun

Here Comes the Sun / Oh Darling

Angola	Parlophone	8E006-04423	1970	Picture	'B' Side
Japan	Apple	AR-2520	1970	Picture	'B' Side
Japan	Apple	EAR-20252	1977	Picture	'B' Side
Portugal	Parlophone	8E006-04423	1970	Picture	'B' Side

Here Comes the Sun / Octopus' Garden

USA	Capitol J/Box	S7-17700 (Orange)	1994-96	Company	'A' Side

Here, There and Everywhere

Here, There and Everywhere / Good Day Sunshine

India	Parlophone	45-DPE.190	1966	Company	'A' Side
USA	Capitol J/Box	S7-18897 (Orange)	1994-96	Company	'A' Side

Here, There and Everywhere / Taxman

Philippines	Parlophone	PAL 60617	1967	Company	'B' Side

Hey Bulldog

Hey Bulldog / All Together Now

France	Apple	006-04982	1972	Picture	'B' Side
France	Apple	2C-10 04982	1976	Company	'B' Side
W Germany	Apple	2C-10 04982	1969	Picture	'B' Side
Italy	Parlophone	006-04462	1976	Company	'B' Side
Sweden	Apple	006-04982	1972	Picture	'B' Side

Hey Jude

Hey Jude / Revolution

Australia	Parlophone	A8493	1968	Company	'A' Side
Brazil	EMI	45BT 97	19?	Picture	'A' Side
Canada	Apple	2276	1968	Company	'A' Side
Chile	Odeon	MSOD 8769	1968	Company	'A' Side
Denmark	Apple	DP 570	1968	Picture	'A' Side
Denmark	Parlophone	DP 570	1968	Picture	'A' Side
Ecuador	Odeon	87789	1968	Company	'A' Side
France	Odeon	FOS 127	1968	Picture	'A' Side
France	Apple	FOS 127	1968	Picture	'A' Side
France	Apple	APF 504	1968	Picture	'A' Side
Finland	Parlophone	DP570	1968	Company	'A' Side
Greece	Parlophone	GMSP 134	1968	Company	'A' Side
W Germany	Odeon	23 880	1968	Picture	'A' Side
W Germany	Apple	0 23 880	1968	Company	'A' Side
India	Parlophone	DP 570	1968	Company	'A' Side
India	Apple	DP 570	1968	Company	'A' Side
Ireland	Parlophone	DP (I) 570	1968	Company	'A' Side
Ireland	Apple	DP (I) 570	1968	Company	'A' Side
Israel	Parlophone	DP 570	1968	Picture	'A' Side
Israel	Apple	DP 570	1968	Company	'A' Side
Italy	Parlophone	QMSP 16433	1968	Picture	'A' Side
Italy	Apple	QMSP 16433	1968	Picture	'A' Side
Italy	Parlophone	DP 570	1968	Picture	'A' Side
Italy	Parlophone	QMSP 16433	1968	Picture	'A' Side
Japan	Apple	AR-2121	1968	Picture	'A' Side
Japan	Odeon	OR-2121	1968	Picture	'A' Side
Japan	Odeon	EAR-20238	1977	Picture	'A' Side

Kenya	Parlophone	DP 570	1968	Company	'A' Side
Lebanon	Parlophone	MOL 19	1968	Company	'A' Side
Mexico	Capitol	6365	1968	Comp. &Pic	'A' Side
Netherlands	Parlophone	DP 570	1968	Picture	'A' Side
Netherlands	Apple	DP 570	1968	Company	'A' Side
New Zealand	Parlophone	NZP 3288	1968	Company	'A' Side
New Zealand	Apple	NZP 3288	1968	Company	'A' Side
Nicaragua	Odeon	O-0302	1968	Company	'B' Side
Norway	Parlophone	DP 570	1968	Picture	'A' Side
Pakistan	Apple	DP 570	1968	Company	'A' Side
Peru	Odeon	10425	1968	Company	'A' Side
Philippines	Parlophone	PAL 60799	1968	Company	'B' Side
Portugal	Parlophone	PDP 5089	1968	Picture	'A' Side
Rhodesia	Parlophone	SPD 477	1968	Company	'A' Side
Singapore	Parlophone	DP 570	1969	Company	'A' Side
S Africa	Parlophone	SPD 477	1968	Company	'A' Side
Spain	Odeon	DSOE 16.740	1968	Picture	'A' Side
Sweden	Parlophone	DP 570	1968	Picture	'A' Side
Sweden	Apple	R5722	1968	Company	'A' Side
Turkey	Odeon	LA 4296	1968	Company	'A' Side
UK	Apple	R5722	1968	Company	'A' Side
UK	Parlophone	DP 570	1968	Company	'A' Side
USA	Apple	2276	1968	Company	'A' Side
USA	CapitolJ/Box	S7-17694(Blue)	1994-96	Company	'A' Side
Venezuela	Parlophone	7 PTM 525	1968	Company	'A' Side
W Indies	Parlophone	DP 570	1968	Company	'A' Side
Yugoslavia	Parl/Jugoton	SP8214	1968	Picture	'A' Side

Hold Me Tight

Hold Me Tight / All My Loving

France	Odeon	MO 20005	1966	Company	'A' Side

Hold Me Tight / I Saw Her Standing There

India	Parlophone	45-DPE.159	1963	Company	'B' Side

Hold Me Tight / I Want To Hold Your Hand

France	Odeon	SO 10099	1963	Picture	'B' Side

Hold Me Tight / Not a Second Time

Nicaragua	Odeon	SO10099	1969	Company	'B' Side
Philippines	Parlophone	O10362	1964	Company	'B' Side

Hold Me Tight / Please Mr. Postman

W Germany	Odeon	22 741	1964	Company	'B' Side

Hold Me Tight / Roll Over Beethoven

Australia	Parlophone	A8107	1964	Company	'B' Side
Netherlands	Odeon	O 127	1964	Company	'B' Side

Honey Don't

Honey Don't /
Everybody's Trying to Be My Baby

Greece	Parlophone	GMSP 75	1964	Company	'B' Side

Honey Don't / I'll Follow the Sun

Philippines	Parlophone	PAL 60287	1964	Company	'A' Side

Honey Don't / Rock and Roll Music

Australia	Parlophone	A8143	1965	Company	'B' Side
Chile	Odeon	MSOD 8505	1965	Company	'B' Side

Honey Pie

Honey Pie / Helter Skelter

Venezuela	Parlophone	7 PMT 534	1968	Company	'B' Side

I Am the Walrus

I Am the Walrus / Hello, Goodbye

Australia	Parlophone	A8273	1967	Company	'B' Side
Belgium	Parlophone	R5655	1967	Picture	'B' Side
Brazil	EMI	45BT 95	19?	Picture	'B' Side
Canada	Capitol	2056	1967	Comp & Pic	'B' Side
Canada	Capitol	Target 2056	1969-71	Company	'B' Side
Chile	Odeon	MSOD 8719	1967	Company	'B' Side
Congo	Parlophone	R5655	1967	Picture	'B' Side
Denmark	Parlophone	R5655	1967	Picture	'B' Side
France	Parlophone	R5655	1967	Picture	'B' Side
France	Odeon	FOS 106	1967	Picture	'B' Side
Finland	Parlophone	R5655	1967	Picture	'B' Side
Greece	Parlophone	GMSP 122	1967	Company	'B' Side
W Germany	Odeon	23 660	1967	Picture	'B' Side
India	Parlophone	45-R.5655	1967	Company	'A' Side
Ireland	Parlophone	R(I)5655	1967	Company	'B' Side
Italy	Parlophone	QMSP 16415	1967	Picture	'B' Side
Japan	Apple	AR-1838	1968	Picture	'B' Side
Japan	Odeon	OR-1838	1968	Picture	'B' Side
Japan	Odeon	EAR-20236	1977	Picture	'B' Side
Kenya	Parlophone	R 5655	1967	Company	'B' Side
Lebanon	Parlophone	MOL 10	1967	Company	'B' Side
Mexico	Capitol	6275	1967	Picture	'B' Side
Netherlands	Parlophone	R5655	1967	Picture	'B' Side
New Zealand	Parlophone	NZP 3249	1967	Company	'B' Side
Nicaragua	Odeon	O-0206	1967	Company	'A' Side

Norway	Parlophone	R5655	1967	Picture	'B' Side
Peru	Odeon	10143	1967	Company	'B' Side
Philippines	Parlophone	PAL 60714	1967	Company	'B' Side
Portugal	Parlophone	PDP 5083	1967	Company	'B' Side
Rhodesia	Parlophone	SPD 442	1967	Company	'B' Side
Singapore	Parlophone	R5655	1967	Company	'B' Side
S Africa	Parlophone	SPD 442	1967	Comp & Pic	'B' Side
Spain	Odeon	DSOL 66.082	1967	Picture	'B' Side
Spain	Odeon	1J006-04477	1970	Picture	'B' Side
Sweden	Parlophone	R5655	1967	Picture	'B' Side
Turkey	Odeon	LA 4284	1967	Company	'B' Side
UK	Parlophone	R5655	1967	Company	'B' Side
USA	Capitol	2056	1967	Picture	'B' Side
USA	Capitol	Target 2056	1969	Company	'B' Side

I Call Your Name

I Call Your Name / Long Tall Sally

Brazil	EMI	451 3394	19?	Picture	'A' Side
Denmark	Odeon	DK 1622	1964	Picture	'B' Side
Ecuador	Odeon	87413	1964	Company	'B' Side
Finland	Parlophone	DPY 667	1964	Company	'B' Side
W Germany	Odeon	22 745	1964	Picture	'B' Side
India	Parlophone	45-DPE.164	1963	Company	'B' Side
Japan	Odeon	OR-1155	1965	Picture	'B' Side
Japan	Apple	AR-1155	1965	Picture	'B' Side
Japan	Apple	EAR-20248	1977	Picture	'B' Side
Netherlands	Odeon	O 126	1964	Company	'B' Side
New Zealand	Parlophone	NZP 3166	1964	Company	'B' Side
Norway	Odeon	DK 1622	1964	Picture	'B' Side
Sweden	Odeon	SD 5967	1964	Picture	'B' Side

I Call Your Name / Matchbox

Chile	Odeon	MSOD 8485	1964	Picture	'B' Side

I Don't Want to Spoil the Party

I Don't Want to Spoil the Party / Eight Days a Week

Canada	Capitol	5371	1965	Comp. & Pic	'B' Side
Canada	Capitol	Target 5371	1969-71	Company	'B' Side
Greece	Parlophone	GMSP 82	1965	Picture	'B' Side
Mexico	Musart	3821	1965	Company	'B' Side
USA	Capitol	5371	1965	Picture	'B' Side
USA	Capitol	Target 5371	1969	Company	'B' Side
USA	Capitol	5371	1971	Picture	'B' Side

I Don't Want to Spoil the Party / Everybody's Trying to Be My Baby

Japan	Odeon	OR-1195	1965	Picture	'A' Side
Japan	Apple	AR-1195	1965	Picture	'A' Side
Japan	Odeon	EAS-17061	?	Picture	'A' Side

I Don't Want to Spoil the Party / I'll Follow the Sun

Norway	Odeon	SD 5981	1965	Picture	'B' Side
Sweden	Parlophone	SD 5981	1965	Company	'B' Side

I Don't Want to Spoil the Party / Kansas City

WGermany	Odeon	22 999	1965		Picture	'B' Side

I Don't Want to Spoil the Party / Ticket to Ride

France	Odeon	SO 10129	1965		Picture	'B' Side

I Don't Want to Spoil the Party / Words of Love

Philippines	Parlophone	PAL 60338	1965		Company	'A' Side

I Feel Fine

I Feel Fine / If I Fell

Peru	Odeon	9110	1964	Company	'A' Side

I Feel Fine / Kansas City

Italy	Parlophone	QMSP 16372	1964	Picture	'A' Side

I FEEL FINE / SHE'S A WOMAN

Australia	Parlophone	A8133	1964	Company	'A' Side
Belgium	Parlophone	R5200	1964	Picture	'B' Side
Brazil	EMI	451 3395	19?	Picture	'A' Side
Canada	Capitol	5327	1964	Comp. & Pic	'A' Side
Canada	Capitol	Target 5327	1969-71	Company	'A' Side
Chile	Odeon	MSOD 8500	1964	Picture	'A' Side
Denmark	Parlophone	R5200	1964	Picture	'A' Side
France	Odeon	SO 10125	1964	Picture	'A' Side
Finland	Parlophone	DPY674	1964	Company	'A' Side
Greece	Parlophone	GMSP 65	1964	Company	'A' Side
W Germany	Odeon	22 851	1964	Picture	'A' Side
India	Parlophone	45-R.5200	1964	Company	'A' Side
Ireland	Parlophone	R (I)5200	1964	Company	'A' Side
Israel	Parlophone	R5200	1964	Company	'A' Side
Japan	Odeon	OR-1179	1965	Picture	'A' Side
Japan	Apple	AR-1179	1965	Picture	'A' Side
Japan	Odeon	EAR-20228	1977	Picture	'A' Side
Mexico	Musart	3764	1964	Company	'A' Side

Netherlands	Parlophone	R5200	1964	Picture	'A' Side
New Zealand	Parlophone	NZP 3175	1964	Company	'A' Side
Norway	Parlophone	R5200	1964	Picture	'A' Side
Rhodesia	Parlophone	SPD 341	1964	Company	'A' Side
S Africa	Parlophone	SPD 341	1964	Company	'A' Side
Spain	Odeon	DSOL 66.046	1964	Picture	'A' Side
Sweden	Parlophone	R5200	1964	Picture	'A' Side
Turkey	Odeon	LA 4167	1964	Picture	'A' Side
UK	Parlophone	R5200	1964	Company	'A' Side
USA	Capitol	5327	1964	Picture	'A' Side
USA	Capitol	Target 5327	1969	Company	'A' Side

I Need You

I Need You / Another Girl

| Philippines | Parlophone | PAL 60395 | 1965 | Company | 'A' Side |

I Need You / Dizzy Miss Lizzy

| Italy | Parlophone | QMSP 16385 | 1965 | Picture | 'A' Side |
| Italy | Parlophone | 3C-006 04455 | 1976 | Company | 'A' Side |

I Need You / Help

| Ecuador | Odeon | 87545 | 1965 | Company | 'B' Side |
| Mexico | Capitol | 6011 | 1965 | Company | 'B' Side |

I Saw Her Standing There

I Saw Her Standing There / All My Loving

Chile	Odeon	MSOD 8498	1964	Picture	'A' Side
Finland	Parlophone	DPY 659	1964	Company	'B' Side
Norway	Parlophone	SD 5958	1964	Picture	'B' Side
Sweden	Odeon	SD 5958	1964	Picture	'B' Side

I Saw Her Standing There / Boys

Philippines	Parlophone	PAL 60101	1963	Company	'A' Side

I Saw Her Standing There / Don't Bother Me

France	Odeon	SO 10107	1963	Picture	'A' Side

I Saw Her Standing There / From Me to You

Japan	Odeon	OR-1077	1964	Picture	'B' Side
Japan	Apple	AR-1077	1964	Picture	'B' Side
Japan	Odeon	EAS-17054	?	Picture	'B' Side
Philippines	Parlophone	EGx 883	1963	Company	'B' Side

I Saw Her Standing There / Hold Me Tight

India	Parlophone	45-DPE.159	1963	Company	'A' Side

137

I Saw Her Standing There /
I Want to Hold Your Hand

Canada	Capitol	5112	1964	Company	'B' Side
Canada	Capitol	5112	1969-71	Company	'B' Side
Jamaica	Capitol	?	1965	Picture	'B' Side
USA	Capitol	5112	1963	Picture	'B' Side
USA	Capitol	Target 5112	1969	Company	'B' Side
USA	Capitol	5112	1994	Picture	'B' Side

I Saw Her Standing There /
Little Child

Greece	Parlophone	GMSP 52	1964	Company	'A' Side

I Saw Her Standing There /
Love Me Do

Australia	Parlophone	A 8105	1964	Company	'B' Side
New Zealand	Parlophone	NZP 3154	1964	Company	'B' Side
Turkey	Odeon	LA 4142	1964	Picture	'A' Side

I Saw Her Standing There / Matchbox

Netherlands	Parlophone	HHR 134	1964	Picture	'A' Side
W Germany	Odeon	22 820	1964	Company	'B' Side

I Saw Her Standing There / Misery

Denmark	Odeon	DK 1615	1964	Picture	'A' Side
Nigeria	Parlophone	45-DPN 303	1964	Company	'A' Side

I Saw Her Standing There /
Roll Over Beethoven

| Rhodesia | Parlophone | 45-SPD 299 | 1963 | Company | 'A' Side |
| S Africa | Parlophone | 45 SPD 299 | 1964 | Company | 'A' Side |

Please note that the title 'I Saw Her Standing There' was mistakenly wrongly labelled as 'Just Seventeen' by the S African and Rhodesian record manufacturer.

I Saw Her Standing There /
She Loves You

| Mexico | Musart | 3576 | 1964 | Company | 'B' Side |

I Saw Her Standing There /
Till There Was You

| France | Odeon | SO 10107 | 1964 | Picture | 'A' Side |
| France | Odeon | MO 20006 | 1966 | Company | 'A' Side |

I Saw Her Standing There /
Twist and Shout

| Peru | Odeon | 8920 | 1964 | Company | 'A' Side |

I Should Have Known Better

I Should Have Known Better / A Hard Day's Night

Brazil	EMI	451 3398	19?	Picture	'B' Side
Canada	Capitol	5222	1964	Comp & Pict	'B' Side
Canada	Capitol	Target 5222	1969-71	Company	'B' Side
Chile	Odeon	MSOD 8464	1964	Company	'B' Side
Ecuador	Odeon	87430	1964	Company	'B' Side
France	Odeon	FOS 20.050	1967	Company	'B' Side
Peru	Odeon	9071	1964	Company	'A' Side
USA	Capitol	5222	1964	Picture	'B' Side
USA	Capitol	5222	1969	Company	'B' Side

I Should Have Known Better / And I Love Her

Finland	Parlophone	DPY 672	1964	Company	'A' Side
Greece	Parlophone	GMSP 64	1964	Company	'A' Side
W Germany	Odeon	22 792	1964	Picture	'B' Side
New Zealand	Parlophone	NZP 3172	1964	Company	'A' Side
Norway	Odeon	ND 7436	1964	Picture	'A' Side
Philippines	Parlophone	PAL 60218	1964	Company	'A' Side

I Should Have Known Better / Any Time at All

Mexico	Musart	3721	1964	Company	'A' Side

I Should Have Known Better /
If I Fell

Australia	Parlophone	A 8125	1964	Company	'A' Side
Nigeria	Parlophone	45-DPN.302	1964	Company	'A' Side
Turkey	Odeon	LA 4157	1964	Picture	'A' Side

I Should Have Known Better /
I'll Cry Instead

Japan	Odeon	OR-1139	1964	Picture	'A' Side
Japan	Apple	AR-1139	1964	Picture	'A' Side
Japan	Odeon	EAR-20246	1977	Picture	'A' Side

I Should Have Known Better /
I'm Happy Just to Dance

India	Parlophone	45-DPE.168	1964	Company	'B' Side

I Should Have Known Better /
She Loves You

Chile	Odeon	45/46X4536	1968	Company	'B' Side

I Should Have Known Better /
Tell Me Why

Denmark	Odeon	DK 1624	1964	Picture	'A' Side
Greece	Parlophone	GMSP 57	1964	Picture	'A' Side
Italy	Parlophone	QMSP 16367	1964	Picture	'A' Side
Netherlands	Parlophone	HHR 128	1964	Picture	'A' Side

I Should Have
Known Better / Yesterday

Czech	Supraphon	1 43 2026	1976	Picture	'B' Side
Guatemala	Odeon	4176	1976	Company	'B' Side
Japan	Apple	EAR-20030	1976	Picture	'B' Side
Portugal.	Parlophone	006 06103	1965	Company	'B' Side
S Africa	Parlophone	SPD?	1965	Company	'B' Side
UK	Parlophone	R6013	1976	Picture	'B' Side
Yugoslavia.	Parlophone	88895	1976	Picture	'B' Side

I Should Have Known Better /
You Really Got a Hold on Me

Sweden	Odeon	SD 5971	1964	Picture	'A' Side

I Want to Be Your Man

I Want to Be Your Man /
All My Loving

W Germany	Odeon	22 681	1964	Company	'B' Side
Netherlands	Odeon	O 29504	1964	Company	'B' Side

I Want to Be Your Man /
I Want to Hold Your Hand

Greece	Parlophone	GMSP 45	1964	Picture	'B' Side

I Want to Be Your Man /
Roll Over Beethoven

France	Odeon	SO 10120	1964	Picture	'B' Side

I Want to Be Your Man /
Till There Was You

Philippines	Parlophone	PAL 60270	1964	Company	'A' Side

I Want to Be Your Man /
You Really Got a Hold on Me

Chile	Odeon	MSOD 8525	1965	Picture	'B' Side

I Want to Hold Your Hand

I Want to Hold Your Hand / Hold Me Tight

France	Odeon	SO 10099	1963		Picture	'A' Side

I Want to Hold Your Hand / I'll Get You

Mexico	Musart	3605	1964		Company	'A' Side

I Want to Hold Your Hand / I Saw Her Standing There

Canada	Capitol	5112	1964		Company	'A' Side
Canada	Capitol	5112	1969-71		Company	'A' Side
Jamaica	Capitol	?	1965		Picture	'A' Side
USA	Capitol	5112	1963		Picture	'A' Side
USA	Capitol	Target 5112	1969		Company	'A' Side
USA	Capitol	5112	1994		Picture	'A' Side

I Want to Hold Your Hand / I Want to Be Your Man

Greece	Parlophone	GMSP 45	1964		Company	'A' Side

I Want to Hold Your Hand / Little Child

EGermany	Amiga	SPU 291	1965		Company	'A' Side

I Want to Hold Your Hand / PS I Love You

Italy	Parlophone	QMSP16351	1963		Picture	'B' Side

I Want to Hold Your Hand / Please, Please Me

Philippines	Parlophone	PAL 60102	1963		Company	'A' Side

I Want to Hold Your Hand / Roll Over Beethoven

WGermany	Odeon	22 623	1963		Company	'A' Side

I Want to Hold Your Hand / She Loves You

Brazil	EMI	451 3393	19?		Picture	'B' Side
Prague	Odeon	71-3049	1964		Picture	'A' Side
Spain	Odeon	DSOL 66.056	1964		Company	'B' Side

I Want to Hold Your Hand / This Boy

Australia	Parlophone	A 8103	1963	Company	'A' Side
Chile	Odeon	MSOD 8420	1963	Picture	'A' Side
Denmark	Parlophone	R5084	1963	Picture	'A' Side
Ecuador	Odeon	87361	1964	Company	'A' Side
Finland	Parlophone	DPY 655	1964	Company	'A' Side

India	Parlophone	45-R5084	1963	Company	'A' Side
Ireland	Parlophone	R(I)5084	1963	Company	'A' Side
Japan	Odeon	OR-1041	1963	Picture	'A' Side
Japan	Apple	AR-1041	1963	Picture	'A' Side
Japan	Odeon	EAR-20225	1977	Picture	'A' Side
Netherlands	Parlophone	R5084	1963	Company	'A' Side
New Zealand	Parlophone	NZP 3152	1963	Company	'A' Side
Nigeria	Parlophone	45-R5084	1963	Company	'A' Side
Norway	Parlophone	R5084	1963	Picture	'A' Side
Pakistan	Parlophone	R5084	1964	Company	'A' Side
Peru	Odeon	8856	1963	Company	'A' Side
Sweden	Parlophone	R5084	1963	Picture	'A' Side
S Africa	Parlophone	SPD 293	1963	Company	'A' Side
Turkey	Odeon	LA 4138	1963	Picture	'A' Side
UK	Parlophone	R5084	1963	Company	'A' Side
USA	Capitol	S7-17689 (Crystal)	1994-96	Company	'A' Side

I Will

I Will / Ob-La-De, Ob-La-Da

Philippines	Parlophone	PAL 60838	1968	Company	'B' Side

I, Me, Mine

I, Me, Mine /
The Long and Winding Road

Venezuela	Apple	AP 1804	1970	Company	'B' Side

If I Fell

If I Fell / And I Love Her

Canada	Capitol	5235	1964	Company	'B' Side
Canada	Capitol	5235	1967	Company	'B' Side
Canada	Capitol	Target 5235	1969-71	Company	'B' Side
Chile	Odeon	MSOD 8459	1964	Company	'B' Side
Greece	Parlophone	GMSP 63	1964	Company	'B' Side
India	Parlophone	45-DPE.167	1964	Company	'A' Side
Italy	Parlophone	QMSP 16365	1964	Picture	'B' Side
Italy	Apple	3C006-04108	1964	Picture	'A' Side
Japan	Odeon	OR-1145	1964	Picture	'B' Side
Japan	Apple	AR-1145	1964	Picture	'B' Side
Japan	Odeon	EAR-20247	1977	Picture	'B' Side
Mexico	Musart	3761	1964	Company	'B' Side
Netherlands	Parlophone	HHR 130	1964	Picture '	A' Side
USA	Capitol	5235	1964	Picture '	'B' Side
USA	Capitol	Target 5235	1969	Company	'B' Side

If I Fell / I Feel Fine

Peru	Odeon	9110	1964	Company	'B' Side

If I Fell / I'm Happy Just to Dance with You

Finland	Parlophone	DPY 671	1964	Company	'A' Side
Philippines	Parlophone	PAL 60217	1964	Company	'B' Side

If I Fell / I Should Have Known Better

Australia	Parlophone	A 8125	1964	Company	'B' Side
Nigeria	Parlophone	45-DPN.302	1964	Company	'B' Side
Turkey	Odeon	LA 4157	1964	Company	'B' Side

If I Fell / Rock and Roll Music

Sweden	Parlophone	SD5974	1965	Picture	'B' Side

If I Fell / Tell Me Why

W Germany	Odeon	22 797	1964	Company	'A' Side
Norway	Parlophone	DP 562	1964	Company	'A' Side
UK	Parlophone	DP 562	1964	Company	'A' Side

If I Needed Someone

If I Needed Someone / Girl

Philippines	Parlophone	PAL 60527	1967	Company	'B' Side

If I Needed Someone / Norwegian Wood

USA	Capitol	S7-18888 (Green)	1994-96	Company	'B' Side
USA	Capitol	S7-19341 (Black)	1994-96	Company	'B' Side

I'll Be Back

I'll Be Back / I'll Cry Instead

Philippines	Parlophone	PAL 60220	1964	Company	'B' Side

I'll Be Back / Love Me Do

Mexico	Musart	3722	1964	Company	'B' Side

I'll Cry Instead

I'll Cry Instead / A Taste of Honey

W Germany	Odeon	22 789	1964	Company	'A' Side
Netherlands	Parlophone	HHR 129	1964	Company	'A' Side

I'll Cry Instead / I Should Have Known Better

Japan	Odeon	OR-1139	1964	Picture	'B' Side
Japan	Apple	AR-1139	1964	Picture	'B' Side
Japan	Odeon	EAR-20246	1977	Picture	'B' Side

I'll Cry Instead / I'll Be Back

Philippines	Parlophone	PAL 60220	1964	Company	'A' Side

I'll Cry Instead / I'm Happy Just to Dance with You

Canada	Capitol	5234	1964	Company	'A' Side
Chile	Odeon	MSOD 8466	1964	Company	'A' Side
USA	Capitol	5234	1964	Picture	'A' Side
USA	Capitol	Target 5234	1969	Company	'A' Side

I'll Cry Instead / Matchbox

NewZealand	Parlophone	NZP 3173	1964	Company	'A' Side

I'll Cry Instead / Tell Me Why

India	Parlophone	45-DPE.172	1965	Company	'B' Side

I'll Follow the Sun

I'll Follow the Sun / Eight Days a Week

Chile	Odeon	MSOD 8510	1965	Company	'B' Side

I'll Follow the Sun / Honey Don't

Philippines	Parlophone	PAL 60287	1964	Company	'B' Side

I'll Follow the Sun / I Don't Want to Spoil the Party

Norway	Odeon	SD 5981	1965	Picture	'A' Side
Sweden	Parlophone	SD 5981	1965	Company	'A' Side

I'll Follow the Sun / Kansas City

Japan	Odeon	OR-1194	1964	Picture	'B' Side
Japan	Apple	AR-1194	1964	Picture	'B' Side
Japan	Odeon	EAS-17058	?	Picture	'B' Side

I'll Follow the Sun / Rock and Roll Music

Italy	Parlophone	QMSP 16371	1964	Picture	'B' Side

I'll Follow the Sun / Words of Love

India	Parlophone	45-DPE.180	1965	Company	'A' Side
Kenya	Columbia	45-DPE 180	1965	Company	'A' Side

I'll Get You

I'll Get You / She Loves You

Australia	Parlophone	A8093	1963	Company	'B' Side
Bolivia	Parlophone	R5055	1964	Company	'B' Side
Canada	Capitol	72125	1963	Company	'B' Side
Chile	Odeon	MSOD 8421	1963	Comp.&Pic	'B' Side
Denmark	Parlophone	R5055	1963	Picture	'B' Side
Ecuador	Odeon	87360	1964	Company	'B' Side
Finland	Parlophone	DPY 653	1963	Company	'B' Side
Greece	Parlophone	GMSP 42	1963	Company	'B' Side
WGermany	Odeon	22 554	1963	Company	'B' Side
India	Parlophone	45-R.5055	1963	Company	'B' Side
Ireland	Parlophone	R (I)5055	1963	Company	'B' Side
Italy	Parlophone	QMSP 16347	1963	Picture	'B' Side
Italy	Parlophone	PFC 7501	1963	Company	'B' Side
Japan	Odeon	OR-1058	1964	Picture	'B' Side
Japan	Apple	AR-1058	1964	Picture	'B' Side
Japan	Odeon	EAR-20224	1977	Picture	'B' Side
Netherlands	Parlophone	R5055	1963	Company	'B' Side
NewZealand	Parlophone	NZP 3148	1963	Company	'B' Side
Nigeria	Parlophone	45-R5055 NI	1963	Company	'B' Side
Norway	Parlophone	R5055	1963	Picture	'B' Side
Pakistan	Parlophone	R5055	1963	Company	'B' Side
Peru	Odeon	8806	1963	Company	'B' Side
Philippines	Parlophone	PAL 60106	1963	Company	'B' Side
S Africa	Parlophone	SPD 278	1963	Company	'B' Side
Sweden	Parlophone	R5055	1963	Picture	'B' Side
Turkey	Odeon	LA 4136	1963	Comp &Pic	'B' Side
UK	Parlophone	R5055	1963	Company	'B' Side

USA	Swan	4152	1963	Comp &Pic	'B' Side
USA	Capitol J/Box	S717688(Red)	1994-96	Company	'B' Side

I'll Get You /
I Want to Hold Your Hand

Mexico	Musart	3605	1964	Company	'B' Side

I'll Get You / Sie Liebt Dich

Canada.	Capitol	72162	1964	Company	'B' Side
USA	Swan	4182	1964	Company	'B' Side

I'll Get You / This Boy

France	Odeon	SO 10117	1964	Picture	'B' Side

I'm a Loser

I'm a Loser / Eight Days a Week

India	Parlophone	45-DPE.178	1965	Company	'A' Side
Italy	Parlophone	QMSP 16377	1965	Picture	'B' Side

I'm a Loser / Mr. Moonlight

Philippines	Parlophone	PAL 60284	1964	Company	'B' Side

I'm a Loser / Rock and Roll Music

Belgium	Odeon	MO 20007	1965	Picture	'B' Side
France	Odeon	MO 20007	1966	Company	'B' Side
W Germany	Odeon	22 915	1965	Picture	'B' Side
Switzerland	Odeon	9 922 915	1965	Picture	'B' Side

I'm Down

I'm Down / Help

Australia	Parlophone	A8163	1965	Company	'B' Side
Belgium	Parlophone	R5305	1965	Picture	'B' Side
Brazil	EMI	451 3399	19?	Picture	'B' Side
Canada	Capitol	5476	1965	Comp. & Pic	'B' Side
Canada	Capitol	2056	1969	Company	'B' Side
Chile	Odeon	MSOD 8535	1965	Company	'B' Side
Congo	HMV	R5305	1965	Company	'B' Side
Denmark	Parlophone	R5305	1965	Picture	'B' Side
France	Odeon	SO 10130	1965	Picture	'B' Side
Finland	Parlophone	DPY 684	1965	Company	'B' Side
Guatemala	Odeon	4256	1976	Picture	'B' Side
Greece	Parlophone	GMSP 79	1965	Company	'B' Side
W Germany	Odeon	23 023	1965	Picture	'B' Side
India	Parlophone	45-R.5305	1965	Company	'B' Side
Ireland	Parlophone	R(I)5305	1965	Company	'B' Side
Italy	Parlophone	QMSP 16383	1965	Picture	'B' Side
Japan	Apple	AR-1412	1965	Picture	'B' Side
Japan	Odeon	OR-1412	1965	Picture	'B' Side
Japan	Odeon	EAR-20230	1977	Picture	'B' Side
Netherlands	Parlophone	R5305	1965	Picture	'B' Side
New Zealand	Parlophone	NZP 3187	1965	Company	'B' Side
Nigeria	Parlophone	45-R.5305	1965	Company	'B' Side
Norway	Parlophone	R5305	1965	Picture	'B' Side
Peru	Odeon	9329	1965	Company	'B' Side
Philippines	Parlophone	PAL 60376	1965	Company	'B' Side

Rhodesia	Parlophone	SPD 363	1965	Company	'B' Side
S Africa	Parlophone	SPD 363	1965	Company	'B' Side
Sweden	Parlophone	R5305	1965	Picture	'B' Side
Switzerland	Odeon	9 923 023	1965	Picture	'B' Side
Turkey	Odeon	LA 4221	1965	Picture	'B' Side
UK	Parlophone	R5305	1965	Company	'B' Side
USA	Capitol	5476	1965	Picture	'B' Side
USA	Capitol	Target 5476	1969	Company	'B' Side
USA	Capitol J/Box	S7-17691(White)	1994-96	Company	'B' Side

I'm Happy Just to Dance with You

I'm Happy Just to Dance /
And I Love Her

Turkey	Odeon	LA 4158	1964	Picture	'A' Side

I'm Happy Just to Dance /
I'll Cry Instead

Canada	Capitol	5234	1964	Company	'B' Side
Chile	Odeon	MSOD 8466	1964	Company	'B' Side
USA	Capitol	5234	1964	Picture	'B' Side
USA	Capitol	Target 5234	1969	Company	'B' Side

I'm Happy Just to Dance / If I Fell

Philippines	Parlophone	PAL 60217	1964	Company	'A' Side
Finland	Parlophone	DPY 671	1964	Company	'B' Side

I'm Happy Just to Dance /
I Should Have Known Better

India	Parlophone	45-DPE.168	1964	Company	'A' Side

I'm Happy Just to Dance /
Movie Medley

Australia	Parlophone	2C008.07627	1982	Company	'B' Side
Canada.	Capitol	B-510o	1982	Company	'A' Side
Canada.	Capitol	B-5107	1982	Comp &Pict	'A' Side

French	Parlophone	R.6055	1982	Picture	'B' Side
Guatemala	Odeon	4601	1982	Picture	'B' Side
W Germany	Odeon	1C-006-07627	1982	Picture	'A' Side
Mexico	EMI	8667	1982	Picture	'A' Side
Netherlands	Parlophone	R.6055	1982	Picture	'B' Side
New Zealand	Parlophone	NZP3583	1982	Picture	'B' Side
Ecuador	Odeon	102-0152	1982	Picture	'B' Side
Japan	Odeon	EAS-17226	1982	Picture	'A' Side
Peru.	Odeon	01.01.1951	1982	Company	'A' Side
UK	Parlophone	R.6055	1982	Picture	'A' Side
USA	Capitol	B-5100	1982	Company	'A' Side
USA	Capitol	B-5107	1982	Comp &Pict	'A' Side

I'm Happy Just to Dance /
Slow Down

W Germany	Odeon	22 838	1964	Company	'B' Side

I'm Happy Just to Dance /
Tell Me Why

Japan	Odeon	OR-1172	1965	Picture	'A' Side
Japan	Apple	AR-1172	1965	Picture	'A' Side
Japan	Odeon	EAS-17057	?	Picture	'A' Side

I'm Happy Just to Dance /
Things We Said Today

France	Odeon	SO 10122	1965	Picture	'A' Side

I'm Looking Through You

I'm Looking Through You /
What Goes On

India	Parlophone	45DPE.193	1970	Company	'A' Side
Philippines	Parlophone	PAL 60472	1967	Company	'A' Side
S Africa	Parlophone	SDP 390	1966	Company	'B' Side

In My Life

In My Life / Run for Your Life

Philippines	Parlophone	PAL 60471	1966	Company	'B' Side

It Won't Be Long

It Won't Be Long / All My Loving

| France | Odeon | SO 10100 | 1963 | Picture | 'B' Side |

It Won't Be Long / Devil in Her Heart

| E Germany | Amiga | 450493 | 1965 | Picture | 'A' Side |

It Won't Be Long / Love Me Do

| Philippines | Parlophone | PAL 60263 | 1964 | Company | 'B'Side |

It Won't Be Long / Money

| W Germany | Odeon | 22 638 | 1964 | Company | 'A' Side |
| Netherlands | Odeon | O 29499 | 1963 | Company | 'A' Side |

It's All Too Much

It's All Too Much / Only a Northern Song

| USA | CapitolJ/Box | S718893(Blue) | 1994-96 | Company | 'A' Side |

It's Only Love

It's Only Love / Act Naturally

Philippines	Parlophone	PAL60394	1965	Company	'B' Side

I've Just Seen a Face

I've Just Seen a Face / Tell Me What You See

Philippines	Parlophone	PAL 60393	1965	Company	'B' Side

I've Just Seen a Face / You've Got to Hide Your Love Away

USA	CapitolJ/Box	S718889(Orange)	1994-96	Company	'B' Side

Julia

Julia / Ob-La-De, Ob-La-Da

USA	Capitol	4347	1976	Company	'B' Side
USA	Capitol J/Box	S718900 (Crystal)	1994	Company	'B' Side

Just Seventeen

Just Seventeen / Roll Over Beethoven

Rhodesia	Parlophone	SPD 299	1964	Comp.& Pict	'A' Side
S Africa	Parlophone	SPD 299	1964	Comp.& Pict	'A' Side

Please note that the title 'Just Seventeen' was a mistake by the S African record manufacturer, it should have read 'I saw her standing there' which is the correct title of the song

Kansas City

Kansas City / Boys

Canada	Capitol	Starline 45-6066	1965	Company	'A' Side
USA	Capitol	Starline 6066	1965	Company	'B' Side
USA	Capitol	Target 6066	1969	Company	'B' Side

Kansas City / I Don't Want to Spoil the Party

WGermany	Odeon	22 999	1965	Company	'A' Side

Kansas City / I Feel Fine

Italy	Parlophone	QMSP 16372	1964	Picture	'B' Side

Kansas City / I'll Follow the Sun

Japan	Odeon	OR 1194	1965	Picture	'A' Side
Japan	Apple	AR 1194	1965	Picture	'A' Side
Japan	Odeon	EAS 17060	1977	Picture	'A' Side

Komm Gib Mir Deine Hand

Komm Gib Mir Deine Hand / Sie Liebt Dich

Australia	Parlophone	A 8117	1964	Company	'A' Side
W Germany	Odeon	22 671	1964	Picture	'A' Side
W Germany	Odeon	1C006-04204	1969	Picture	'A' Side

Lady Madonna

Lady Madonna / The Inner Light

Australia	Parlophone	A8293	1968	Company	'A' Side
Belgium	Parlophone	R5675	1968	Picture	'A' Side
Canada	Capitol	2138	1969	Comp & Pict	'A' Side
Chile	Odeon	MSOD 8725	1968	Picture	'A' Side
Denmark	Parlophone	R5675	1968	Picture	'A' Side
Ecuador	Odeon	87754	1968	Company	'A' Side
France	Odeon	FO 111	1968	Picture	'A' Side
Finland	Parlophone	R5675	1968	Company	'A' Side
Greece	Parlophone	GMSP 129	1968	Company	'A' Side
W Germany	Odeon	23 733	1968	Picture	'A' Side
India	Parlophone	45-R.5675	1968	Company	'A' Side
Ireland	Parlophone	R (I) 5675	1968	Company	'A' Side
Israel	Parlophone	R5675	1968	Picture	'A' Side
Italy	Parlophone	QMSP 16423	1968	Picture	'A' Side
Italy	Parlophone	R5675	1968	Company	'A' Side
Japan	Odeon	OR-1902	1968	Picture	'A' Side

Japan	Apple	AR-1902	1968	Picture	'A' Side
Japan	Odeon	EAR-20237	1977	Picture	'A' Side
Kenya	Parlophone	R5675	1968	Company	'A' Side
Lebanon	Parlophone	MOL.13	1968	Company	'A' Side
Mexico	Capitol	6310	1968	Picture	'A' Side
Netherlands	Parlophone	R5675	1968	Picture	'A' Side
New Zealand	Parlophone	NZP 3265	1968	Company	'A' Side
Norway	Parlophone	R5675	1968	Picture	'A' Side
Pakistan	Parlophone	R5675	1968	Company	'A' Side
Peru	Odeon	10274	1968	Company	'A' Side
Philippines	Parlophone	PAL 60752	1968	Company	'A' Side
Portugal	Parlophone	PDP 5085	1968	Company	'A' Side
Rhodesia	Parlophone	SPD 386	1966	Company	'A' Side
S Africa	Parlophone	SPD 456	1968	Company	'A' Side
Singapore	Parlophone	R5675	1968	Company	'A' Side
Spain	Odeon	DSOL 66.086	1968	Picture	'A' Side
Spain	Odeon	1J006-04478	1970	Picture	'A' Side
Sweden	Parlophone	R5675	1968	Picture	'A' Side
Turkey	Odeon	LA 4286	1968	Company	'A' Side
UK	Parlophone	R5675	1968	Company	'A' Side
USA	Capitol	2138	1968	Picture	'A' Side
USA	Capitol	Target 2138	1969	Company	'A' Side
Venezuela	Parlophone	7PMT 524	1968	Company	'A' Side
W Indies	Parlophone	Stateside R5675	1968	Company	'A' Side
Yugoslavia	Parl/Jugoton	SPP8175	1968	Picture	'A' Side

Let It Be

Let It Be /
You Know My Name, Look up the Number

Australia	Apple	A9083	1970	Picture	'A' Side
Brazil	EMI	45BT 102	19?	Picture	'A' Side
Brazil	Apple	7-BT-31	1970	Picture	'A' Side
Canada	Apple	2764	1970	Comp. &Picture	'A' Side
Chile	Apple	Apple 13	1970	Company	'A' Side
Denmark	Apple	R5833	1970	Picture	'A' Side
Ecuador	Odeon	87902	1970	Company	'A' Side
France	Apple	2C006-04353	1970	Picture	'A' Side
Greece	Parlophone	GMSP 147	1970	Company	'A' Side
Guatemala	Odeon	4210	19766	Company	'A' Side
WGermany	Apple	1C006-04353	1970	Picture	'A' Side
India	Apple	45-R.5833	1970	Company	'A' Side
Ireland	Apple	R (I)5833	1970	Picture	'A' Side
Israel	Apple	AP 2764	1970	Picture	'A' Side
Italy	Apple	QMSP 16467	1970	Picture	'A' Side
Italy	Apple	3C006-04353	1970	Picture	'A' Side
Japan	Apple	AR-2461	1970	Picture	'A' Side
Japan	Apple	EAR-20242	1977	Picture	'A' Side
Japan	Odeon	EAR-20501	1981	Picture	'A' Side
Kenya	Parlophone	R 5833	1970	Company	'A' Side
Lebanon	Apple	R58337YCE2147	1970	Company	'A' Side
Malaysia	Apple	R5833	1970	Picture	'A' Side
Mexico	Apple	6645	1970	Picture	'A' Side

Country	Label	Catalogue	Year	Type	Side
Mozambique	Bayal/Parlophone	1 5006	1970	Company	'A' Side
Netherlands	Apple	5C006-04353	1970	Picture	'A' Side
New Zealand	Apple	NZP 3357	1970	Company	'A' Side
Nicaragua	Odeon	O1-0469	1970	Company	'A' Side
Norway	Apple	R5833	1970	Picture	'A' Side
Peru	Apple	10959	1970	Company	'A' Side
Philippines	Apple	PAL 60924	1970	Company	'A' Side
Portugal	Parlophone	8E006-04353	1970	Picture	'A' Side
Rhodesia	Parlophone	SPD 531	1970	Company	'A' Side
S Africa	Parlophone	SPD 531	1970	Company	'A' Side
Singapore	Apple	R5833	1970	Company	'A' Side
Spain	Odeon	1J006-04353	1970	Picture	'A' Side
Sweden	Apple	R5833	1970	Picture	'A' Side
Turkey	Apple	LA 4317	1970	Company	'A' Side
UAR.	Parlophone	7041235	1970	Picture	'A' Side
UK	Parlophone	PR5833	1970	Company	'A' Side
UK	Apple	R5833	1970	Picture	'A' Side
UK	Apple	PR5833	1970	Company	'A' Side
USA	Apple	2764	1970	Picture	'A' Side
USA	Capitol/J/Box	S7-17695(Yellow)	1994-96	Company	'A' Side
Venezuela	Odeon	OD-45-31	1970	Company	'A' Side
W Indies	Parlophone	R5833	1970	Company	'A' Side
Yugoslavia	Apple / Jugoton	SAP 8361	1970	Picture	'A' Side

Let It Be / Get Back

Country	Label	Catalogue	Year	Type	Side
Japan	Odeon	EAR-20501	1981	Picture	'B' Side

Little Child

Little Child /
Do You Want to Know a Secret

W Germany   Odeon   22 710   1964   Company   'B' Side

Little Child /
I Saw Her Standing There

Greece   Parlophone   GMSP 52   1964   Company   'B' Side

Little Child /
I Want to Hold Your Hand

E Germany   Amiga   SPU 291   1964   Company   'B' Side

Long Tall Sally

Long Tall Sally / A Hard Day's Night

Bolivia	Odeon	BO 1055	1964	Company	'B' Side
USA	BeatRecords	2,1964	197?	Picture	'A' Side

Long Tall Sally / I Call Your Name

Brazil	EMI	451 3394	19?	Picture	'B' Side
Denmark	Odeon	DK 1622	1964	Company	'A' Side
Ecuador	Odeon	87413	1964	Picture	'A' Side
Finland	Parlophone	DPY 667	1964	Company	'A' Side
W Germany	Odeon	22 745	1964	Comp & Pict	'A' Side
India	Parlophone	45-DPE.164	1963	Company	'A' Side
Japan	Odeon	OR-1155	1965	Picture	'A' Side
Japan	Apple	AR-1155	1965	Picture	'A' Side
Japan	Odeon	EAR-20248	1977	Picture	'A' Side
Netherlands	Odeon	O 126	1964	Company	'A' Side
New Zealand	Parlophone	NZP 3166	1964	Company	'A' Side
Norway	Odeon	DK 1622	1964	Picture	'A' Side
Sweden	Odeon	SD 5967	1964	Picture	'A' Side

Long Tall Sally / Matchbox

Greece	Parlophone	GMSP 54	1964	Picture	'A' Side

Long Tall Sally / She's a Woman

France	Odeon	2c-010-04457	1978	Picture	'A' Side
Italy	Parlophone	QMSP 16381	1965	Picture	'A' Side

Long Tall Sally / Slow Down

Chile	Odeon	MSOD 8486	1964	Picture	'A' Side

Love Me Do

Love Me Do / PS I Love You

Brazil	EMI	451 3401	19?	Picture	'A' Side
Canada	Capitol	72076	1963	Company	'A' Side
Canada	Capitol	Starline45-6062	1965	Company	'A' Side
Chile	Odeon	MSOD 8431	1964	Company	'A' Side
Finland	Parlophone	DPY 664	1964	Company	'A' Side
India	Parlophone	45-R.4949	1963	Company	'A' Side
Ireland	Parlophone	R(I)4949	1962	Company	'A' Side
Italy	Bluebell	Tollie T9008	1964	Picture	'A' Side
Japan	Odeon	EAS-27005	1982	Picture	'A' Side
Japan	Odeon	TOKP-7085	1992	Picture	'A' Side
Nigeria	Parlophone	45-R4949 NI	1963	Company	'A' Side
Norway	Parlophone	R4949	1964	Picture	'A' Side
Pakistan	Parlophone	R4949	1963	Company	'A' Side
Peru	Odeon	8980	1964	Company	'A' Side
UK	Parlophone	R4949	1962	Company	'A' Side
UK	Parlophone	R4949	1963	Company	'A' Side
USA	Tollie	9008	1964	Picture	'A' Side
USA	Oldies	45 OL 151	1964	Company	'A' Side
USA	Capitol	Starline 6062	1965	Company	'A' Side

Lucy in the Sky with Diamonds

Lucy in the Sky with Diamond /
When I'm Sixty-Four

USA	CapitolJ/Box	S7-18896 (Red)	1994-96	Company	'A' Side

Magical Mystery Tour

Magical Mystery Tour /
Fool on the Hill

USA	CapitolJ/Box	S7-1889(Yellow)	1994-96	Company	'A' Side

Matchbox

Matchbox / I Call Your Name

Chile	Odeon	MSOD 8485	1964	Picture	'A' Side

Matchbox / I'll Cry Instead

NewZealand	Parlophone	NZP 3173	1964	Company	'B' Side

Matchbox / I Saw Her Standing There

W Germany	Odeon	22 820	1964	Company	'A' Side
Netherlands	Parlophone	HHR 134	1964	Picture	'B' Side

Matchbox / Long Tall Sally

Greece	Parlophone	GMSP 54	1964	Picture	'B' Side

Matchbox / Slow Down

Canada	Capitol	5255	1964	Comp.& Pict	'A' Side
Canada	Capitol	Target 5255	1969-71	Company	'A' Side
Japan	Odeon	OR-1156	1964	Picture	'A' Side
Japan	Apple	AR-1156	1964	Picture	'A' Side
Japan	Apple	EAS-17056	?	Picture	'A' Side
Philippines	Parlophone	PAL 60255	1964	Company	'B' Side
USA	Capitol	5255	1964	Picture	'A' Side
USA	Capitol	Target 5255	1969	Company	'B' Side

Matchbox / Words of Love

| Rhodesia | Parlophone | SPD 356 | 1965 | Company | 'B' Side |
| S Africa | Parlophone | SPD 356 | 1965 | Company | 'B' Side |

Maxwell's Silver Hammer

Maxwell's Silver Hammer / Oh Darling

| Nicaragua | Apple | O1-0455 | 1970 | Company | 'A' Side |

Michelle

Michelle / Drive My Car

Belgium	Parlophone	DP 564	1966	Company	'A' Side
Congo	Parlophone	DP 564	1966	Company	'A' Side
Nigeria	Parlophone	45-DP 564	1966	Company	'B' Side
Turkey	Odeon	LA 4252	1966	Picture	'A' Side
UK	Parlophone	DP 564	1966	Company	'A' Side

Michelle / Girl

Denmark	Odeon	SD 5987	1966	Picture	'A' Side
Ecuador	Odeon	87596	1966	Company	'B' Side
Finland	Parlophone	DPY 696	1966	Company	'A' Side
W Germany	Odeon	23 152	1966	Picture	'A' Side
Netherlands	Parlophone	HHR 139	1966	Picture	'A' Side
Norway	Parlophone	SD 5987	1966	Picture	'A' Side
Sweden	Parlophone	SD 5987	1966	Picture	'A' Side
Switzerland	Odeon	9 23 152	1966	Picture	'A' Side

Michelle / Help

Nicaragua	Odeon	O-0360	1969	Picture	'B' Side

Michelle / Nowhere Man

Finland	Parlophone	DPY 698	1966	Company	'A' Side

Michelle / Run for Your Life

France	Odeon	FOS 101	1966	Company	'A' Side
Italy	Parlophone	QMSP16389	1966	Picture	'A' Side

Michelle / The Word

Philippines	Parlophone	PAL 60557	1967	Company	'A' Side

Michelle / Yesterday

Brazil	EMI	45BT 91	19?	Picture	'A' Side

Michelle / You Won't See Me

India	Parlophone	45-DPE 187	1966	Company	'A' Side
W Indies	Capitol	?	1966	Company	'A' Side

Misery

Misery / Anna

| Philippines | Parlophone | PAL 60272 | 1964 | Company | 'A' Side |

Misery / Ask Me Why

| W Germany | Odeon | 22 663 | 1964 | Company | 'A' Side |
| Netherlands | Odeon | O 29501 | 1963 | Company | 'B' Side |

Misery / Can't Buy Me Love

| Chile | Odeon | MSOD 8477 | 1964 | Company | 'B' Side |

Misery / I Saw Her Standing There

| Denmark | Odeon | DK 1615 | 1964 | Picture | 'B' Side |
| Nigeria | Parlophone | 45-DPN 303 | 1964 | Picture | 'B' Side |

Misery / Roll Over Beethoven

| USA | Capitol | Starline 6065 | 1965 | Company | 'B' Side |
| USA | Capitol | Target 6065 | 1969 | Company | 'B' Side |

Misery / Twist and Shout

| Italy | Parlophone | QMSP 16352 | 1964 | Picture | 'B' Side |
| Italy | Parlophone | PFC 7503 | 1966 | Company | 'B' Side |

Money

Money / Do You Want to Know a Secret

New Zealand	Parlophone	NZP 3163	1964	Company	'B' Side

Money / It Won't Be Long

W Germany	Odeon	22 638	1964	Company	'B' Side
Netherlands	Odeon	O 29499	1963	Company	'B' Side

Money / Please Mr. Postman

Japan	Odeon	OR-1102	1964	Picture	'B' Side
Japan	Apple	AR-1102	1964	Picture	'B' Side
Japan	Odeon	EAR-20245	1977	Picture	'B' Side

Movie Medley

Movie Medley /
I'm Happy Just to Dance

Australia	Parlophone	A-689	1982	Company	'A' Side
Austria	Parlophone	2C008.07627	1982	Picture	'A' Side
Canada.	Capitol	B-510o	1982	Company	'B' Side
Canada.	Capitol	B-5107	1982	Comp & Pict	'B' Side
French	Parlophone	R.6055	1982	Picture	'A' Side
Guatemala	Odeon	4601	1982	Company	'A' Side
W Germany	Odeon	IC-006-07027	1982	Picture	'A' Side
Italy	Parlophone	3C-006-07027	1982	Picture	'A' Side
Mexico	Capitol	3C006.07627	1982	Picture	'B' Side
Netherlands.	Parlophone	R.6055	1982	Picture	'A' Side
New Zealand	Parlophone	NZP3583	1982	Picture	'A' Side
Ecuador	Odeon	102-0152	1982	Picture	'A' Side
Japan	Odeon	EAS-17226	1982	Picture	'B' Side
Peru.	Odeon	01.01.1951	1982	Company	'B' Side
UK	Parlophone	R.6055	1982	Picture	'B' Side
USA	Capitol	B-5100	1982	Company	'B' Side
USA	Capitol	B-5107	1982	Comp & Pict	'B' Side

Mr. Moonlight

Mr. Moonlight / I'm a Loser

Philippines	Parlophone	PAL 60284	1964	Company	'A' Side

Mr. Moonlight / What You're Doing

Japan	Odeon	OR-1193	1965	Picture	'A' Side
Japan	Apple	AR-1193	1965	Picture	'A' Side
Japan	Odeon	EAS-17059	?	Picture	'A' Side

No Reply

No Reply / Baby's in Black

Italy	Parlophone	QMSP16370	1964	Picture	'A' Side

No Reply / Eight Days a Week

Ecuador	Odeon	87496	1965	Company	'A' Side
W Germany	Odeon	22 893	1965	Picture	'A' Side
Japan	Odeon	OR-1189	1965	Picture	'A' Side
Japan	Apple	AR-1189	1965	Picture	'A' Side
Japan	Odeon	EAS-17058	1965	Picture	'A' Side
New Zealand	Parlophone	NZP 3179	1964	Company	'B' Side
Switzerland	Odeon	9-922-893	1965	Picture	'A' Side

No Reply / Rock and Roll Music

Greece	Parlophone	GMSP 84	1965	Picture	'B' Side
India	Parlophone	45-DPE.179	1965	Company	'B' Side
Netherlands	Parlophone	HHR 136	1965	Picture	'A' Side
Philippines	Parlophone	PAL 60283	1964	Company	'A' Side

No Reply / What You're Doing

Peru	Odeon	9221	1965	Company	'A' Side

Norwegian Wood

Norwegian Wood / Drive My Car

India	Parlophone	45-DPE.186	1965	Company	'A' Side

Norwegian Wood / If I Needed Someone

USA	CapitolJ/Box	S7-18888 (Green)	1994-96	Company	'B' Side
USA	CapitolJ/Box	S7-18888 (Black)	1994-96	Company	'B' Side

Norwegian Wood / Nowhere Man

Australia	Parlophone	A 8193	1966	Company	'B' Side

Not a Second Time

Not a Second Time / Hold Me Tight

Nicaragua	Odeon	SO 10099	1969	Company	'B' Side
Philippines	Parlophone	PAL 60269	1964	Company	'A' Side

Nowhere Man

Nowhere Man / Drive My Car

S Africa	Parlophone	SPD 381	1966	Company	'A' Side

Nowhere Man / Girl

French	Odeon	2C-10 04474	1976	Company	'B' Side
India	Parlophone	45-DPY.698	1966	Company	'B' Side
Italy	Parlophone	QMSP 16398	1966	Company	'B' Side
Italy	Parlophone	PFC 7507	1966	Company	'A' Side

Nowhere Man / Michelle

Finland	Parlophone	DPY 698	1966	Company	'B' Side

Nowhere Man / Norwegian Wood

Australia	Parlophone	A 8193	1966	Company	'A' Side

Nowhere Man / The Word

France	Odeon	FOS 108	1967	Company	'A' Side

Nowhere Man / What Goes On

Canada	Capitol	5587	1966	Comp & Picture	'A' Side
Canada	Capitol	5587	1969-70	Company	'A' Side
W Germany	Odeon	23 171	1966	Picture	'A' Side
Japan	Odeon	OR-1510	1966	Picture	'A' Side

Japan	Apple	AR-1510	1966	Picture	'A' Side
Japan	Odeon	EAS-17065	?	Picture	'A' Side
Switzerland	Odeon	9 23 171	1966	Picture	'A' Side
USA	Capitol	5587	1966	Picture	'A' Side
USA	Capitol	Target 5587	1969	Company	'A' Side
USA	Capitol J/Box	S7-18894 (Green)	1994-96	Picture	'A' Side

Ob-La-De, Ob-La-Da

Ob-La-Da, Ob-La-De /
Back in the USSR

Italy	Apple	QMSP 16447	1968	Picture	'A' Side

Ob-La-De, Ob-La-Da / Birthday

Peru	Apple	10570	1968	Company	'A' Side

Ob-La-De, Ob-La-Da /
Happiness Is a Warm Gun

Finland	Parlophone	DPY 990	1968	Company	'A' Side

Ob-La-De, Ob-La-Da / I Will

Philippines	Parlophone	PAL 60838	1968	Company	'A' Side

Ob-La-De, Ob-La-Da / Julia

USA	Capitol	4347	1976	Company	'A' Side
USA	Capitol J/Box	S718900(Crystal)	1994-96	Company	'A' Side

Ob-La-De, Ob-La-Da / Oh Darling

S Africa	Parlophone	SPD 573	1970	Company	'A'Side

Ob-La-De, Ob-La-Da / Sexy Sadie

W Indies	Parlophone	?	1968	Company	'A' Side

Ob-La-De, Ob-La-Da /
While My Guitar Gently Weeps

Australia	Apple	A 8693	1969	Company	'A' Side
Brazil	EMI	45BT 98	19?	Picture	'A' Side
Chile	Apple	Apple 5	1968	Company	'A' Side
Ecuador	Odeon	87839	1969	Company	'A' Side
France	Apple	FO 148	1969	Picture	'A' Side
W Germany	Apple	24004	1968	Company	'A' Side
Greece	Parlophone	GMSP 137	1968	Company	'A' Side
India	Parlophone	45-DPE.192	1968	Company	'A' Side
Israel	Apple	FO 148	1968	Picture	'A' Side
Japan	Apple	AR-2207	1969	Picture	'A' Side
Japan	Apple	EAR-20251	1977	Picture	'A' Side
Lebanon	Parlophone	MOL 29	1969	Company	'A' Side
New Zealand	Apple	NZP 3318	1969	Company	'A' Side
Netherlands	Apple	HHR 142	1969	Picture	'A' Side
Philippines	Apple	PAL 60838	1968	Company	'A' Side
Spain	Odeon	OSL-203	1969	Picture	'A' Side
Spain	Odeon	J006-04690	1970	Picture	'A' Side
Turkey	Apple	LA 4302	1968	Company	'A' Side

Ob-La-Da, Ob-La-Da /
Why Don't We Do It in the Road

Nicaragua Odeon   O-0363   1967   Company   'A' Side

Octopus' Garden

Octopus' Garden /
Here Comes the Sun

USA   Capitol J/Box   S7-17700 (Orange) 1994-96 Company 'B' Side

Oh Darling

Oh Darling / Because

Philippines	Parlophone	PAL61152	1969	Company	'A' Side

Oh Darling / Come Together

Venezuela	Odeon	OD-45153	1970	Company	'A' Side

Oh Darling / Here Comes the Sun

Angola	Parlophone	8E 006-04423	1970	Picture	'A' Side
Japan	Apple	AR-2520	1970	Picture	'A' Side
Japan	Apple	EAR-20252	1977	Picture	'A' Side
Portugal	Parlophone	8E 006-04423	1970	Picture	'A' Side

Oh Darling / Maxwell's Silver Hammer

Nicaragua	Apple	O1-0455	1970	Company	'A' Side

Oh Darling / Ob-La-De, Ob-La-Da

S Africa	Parlophone	SPD 573	1970	Company	'B' Side

Old Brown Shoe

Old Brown Shoe /
Ballad of John and Yoko

Australia	Apple	A8793	1969	Company	'B' Side
Brazil	EMI	45BT 100	19?	Picture	'B' Side
Canada	Apple	2531	1969	Comp. & Pic	'B' Side
Chile	Apple	Apple 9	1969	Company	'B' Side
Denmark	Apple	R5786	1969	Picture	'B' Side
Ecuador	Odeon	87828	1969	Company	'B' Side
France	Apple	2C006-04108	1969	Picture	'B' Side
Finland	Apple	R5786	1969	Company	'B' Side
Greece	Parlophone	GMSP 141	1969	Company	'B' Side
W Germany	Apple	1C006-04108	1969	Picture	'B' Side
India	Apple	45-R.5786	1969	Company	'B' Side
Ireland	Apple	R (I) 5786	1969	Company	'B' Side
Israel	Apple	R5786	1969	Picture	'B' Side
Italy	Apple	QMSP 16456	1969	Picture	'B' Side
Italy	Apple	3C006-04108	1969	Picture	'B' Side
Japan	Apple	AR-2301	1969	Picture	'B' Side
Japan	Apple	EAR-20240	1977	Picture	'B' Side
Kenya	Parlophone	R5786	1969	Company	'B' Side
Lebanon	Apple	R5786	1969	Company	'B' Side
Malaysia	Apple	R5786	1969	Company	'B' Side
Mexico	Apple	6510	1969	Picture	'B' Side
Netherlands	Apple	5C006-04108	1969	Picture	'B' Side
New Zealand	Apple	NZP 3329	1969	Company	'B' Side
Norway	Apple	R5786	1969	Picture	'B' Side
Peru	Apple	10717	1969	Company	'B' Side

Philippines	Apple	PAL 60871	1969	Company	'B' Side
Portugal	Parlophone	PDP 5092	1969	Picture	'B' Side
Singapore	Apple	R5786	1969	Company	'B' Side
S Africa	Parlophone	SPD 516	1969	Company	'B' Side
Spain	Odeon	1J006-04108	1969	Picture	'B' Side
Sweden	Apple	R5786	1969	Picture	'B' Side
Turkey	Apple	LA 4310	1969	Company	'B' Side
UK	Apple	R5786	1969	Company	'B' Side
USA	Apple	2531	1969	Picture	'B' Side
Venezuela	Odeon	OD-45-1A	1969	Company	'B' Side
Yugoslavia	Apple / Jugoton	SAP 8304	1969	Company	'B' Side

Only a Northern Song

Only a Northern Song / It's All Too Much

USA	CapitolJ/Box	S7-18893 (Blue)	1994-96	Company	'B' Side

PS I Love You

PS I Love You / Chains

| Philippines | Parlophone | PAL60273 | 1964 | Company | 'A' Side |

PS I Love You / From Me to You

| Sweden | Odeon | SD 5944 | 1963 | Picture | 'B' Side |

PS I Love You / I Want to Hold Your Hand

| Italy | Parlophone | QMSP 16351 | 1963 | Picture | 'A' Side |

PS I Love You / Love Me Do

Brazil	EMI	451 3401	19?	Picture	'B' Side
Canada	Capitol	72076	1963	Company	'B' Side
Canada	Capitol	Starline45-6062	1965	Company	'B' Side
Chile	Odeon	MSOD 8431	1964	Company	'B' Side
Finland	Parlophone	DPY 664	1964	Company	'B' Side
India	Parlophone	45-R.4949	1963	Company	'B' Side
Ireland	Parlophone	R (I)4949	1962	Company	'B' Side
Italy	Bluebell	Tollie T9008	1964	Picture	'B' Side
Japan	Odeon	EAS-27005	1982	Picture	'B' Side
Japan	Odeon	TOKP-7085	1992	Picture	'B' Side
Nigeria	Parlophone	45-R4949 NI	1963	Company	'B' Side
Norway	Parlophone	R4949	1964	Picture	'B' Side
Pakistan	Parlophone	R4949	1964	Company	'B' Side
Peru	Odeon	8980	1964	Company	'B' Side

UK	Parlophone	R4949	1962	Company	'B' Side
UK	Parlophone	R4949	1963	Company	'B' Side
USA	Tollie	9008	1964	Picture	'B' Side
USA	Oldies	45 OL 151	1964	Company	'B' Side
USA	Capitol	Starline 6062	1965	Company	'B' Side
USA	Capitol	B-5189	1982	Picture	'B' Side
USA	Capitol	B-5189	1988	Picture	'B' Side
USA	Capitol	7 PRO 79551/2	1992	Picture	'B' Side
USA	Capitol J/Box	S7-56785 (Red)	1994-96	Company	'B' Side
USA	Capitol J/Box	S7-56785 (Black)	1994-96	Company	'B'

PS I Love You

PS I Love You / Please Mr. Postman

France	Odeon	SO 10112	1964	Picture	'A' Side

PS I Love You / Till There Was You

France	Odeon	SO 10104	1963	Picture	'A' Side

PS I Love You / Twist and Shout

Turkey	Odeon	LA 4143	1964	Picture	'B' Side

Paperback Writer

Paperback Writer / Rain

Australia	Parlophone	A8203	1966	Company	'A' Side
Brazil	EMI	45BT 90	19?	Picture	'A' Side
Canada	Capitol	5651	1966	Comp & Pict	'A' Side
Canada	Capitol	5651	1969-70	Company	'A' Side
Chile	Odeon	MSOD 8606	1966	Company	'A' Side
Denmark	Parlophone	R5452	1966	Picture	'A' Side
France	Odeon	FOS 107	1967	Company	'A' Side
Finland	Parlophone	DPY 699	1966	Company	'A' Side
Greece	Parlophone	GMSP 104	1966	Company	'A' Side
W Germany	Odeon	23 210	1966	Picture	'A' Side
India	Parlophone	45-R.5452	1966	Company	'A' Side
Ireland	Parlophone	R (I)5452	1966	Company	'A' Side
Italy	Parlophone	QMSP 16394	1966	Picture	'A' Side
Japan	Odeon	OR-1529	1966	Picture	'A' Side
Japan	Apple	AR-1529	1966	Picture	'A' Side
Japan	Odeon	EAR-20232	1977	Picture	'A' Side
Mexico	Capitol	6066	1966	Comp & Pic	'A' Side
Netherlands	Parlophone	R5452	1966	Picture	'A' Side
New Zealand	Parlophone	NZP 3204	1966	Company	'A' Side
Nicaragua	Odeon	4O-014	1966	Picture	'A' Side
Nigeria	Parlophone	45-R-5452 NI	1966	Company	'A' Side
Norway	Parlophone	R5452	1966	Picture	'A' Side
Peru	Odeon	9573	1966	Company	'A' Side
Philippines	Parlophone	PAL 60538	1967	Company	'A' Side
Rhodesia	Parlophone	SPD 386	1966	Company	'A' Side
S Africa	Parlophone	SPD 386	1966	Company	'A' Side

Spain	Odeon	DSOL 66.073	1966	Picture	'A' Side
Sweden	Parlophone	R5452	1966	Picture	'A' Side
Switzerland	Odeon	9 23 210	1966	Picture	'A' Side
Turkey	Odeon	LA 4261	1966	Picture	'A' Side
UK	Parlophone	R5452	1966	Company	'A' Side
USA	Capitol	5651	1966	Picture	'A' Side
USA	Capitol	Target 5651	1969	Company	'A' Side
USA	Capitol J/Box	S7-18902(Red)	1994-96	Company	'A' Side
UK	Parlophone	R5452	1966	Company	'A' Side
Yugoslavia.	Parlophone	88923	?	Picture	'A' Side

Penny Lane

Penny Lane / Strawberry Fields

Australia	Parlophone	A8243	1967	Picture	'B' Side
Brazil	Odeon	7-BT-05	1967	Company	'B' Side
Brazil	EMI	45BT-93	19?	Picture	'A' Side
Canada	Capitol	5810	1967	Comp. & Pic	'B' Side
Canada	Capitol	5810	1969-70	Company	'B' Side
Congo	HMV	R5570	1967	Company	'B' Side
Denmark	Parlophone	R5570	1967	Picture	'B' Side
Ecuador	Odeon	87675	1967	Company	'A' Side
France	Odeon	FOS 116	1968	Comp & Pic	'A' Side
France	Odeon	04475	1973	Picture	'A' Side
Finland	Parlophone	R5570	1967	Company	'B' Side
Greece	Parlophone	GMSP 113	1967	Company	'B' Side
W Germany	Odeon	23 436	1967	Picture	'B' Side
India	Parlophone	45-R.5570	1967	Company	'A' Side
Ireland	Parlophone	R (I)5570	1967	Picture	'B' Side
Italy	Parlophone	QMSP 16404	1967	Picture	'B' Side
Japan	Odeon	OR-1685	1967	Picture	'B' Side
Japan	Apple	AR-1685	1967	Picture	'B' Side
Japan	Odeon	EAR-20234	1977	Picture	'B' Side
Mexico	Capitol	6160	1967	Company	'A' Side
Netherlands	Parlophone	R5570	1967	Picture	'B' Side
NewZealand	Parlophone	NZP 3224	1967	Company	'B' Side
Nicaragua	Odeon	O-0172	1967	Company	'B' Side
Nigeria	Parlophone	45-R-5570	1967	Company	'B' Side
Norway	Parlophone	R5570	1967	Picture	'B' Side
Pakistan	Parlophone	R5570	1967	Company	'B' Side

Peru	Odeon	9827	1967	Company	'A' Side
Philippines	Parlophone	PAL 60617	1967	Company	'B' Side
Rhodesia	Parlophone	SPD 415	1967	Company	'B' Side
S Africa	Parlophone	SPD 415	1967	Company	'B' Side
Spain	Odeon	DSOL 66.077	1967	Picture	'B' Side
Spain	Odeon	1J006-04451	1970	Picture	'B' Side
Sweden	Parlophone	R5570	1967	Picture	'B' Side
Switzerland	Odeon	9 23 436	1967	Picture	'B' Side
Turkey	Odeon	LA 4277	1967	Company	'A' Side
UK	Parlophone	R5570	1967	Picture	'B' Side
USA	Capitol	5810	1967	Picture	'A' Side
USA	Capitol	Target 5810	1969	Company	'A' Side
USA	Capitol J/Box	S7-17697 (Red)	1994-96	Company	'A' Side
Venezuela	Odeon	167	1967	Company	'B' Side
Yugoslavia	Parlophone	SPAR58911	1967	Picture	'B' Side

This record was issued as a double 'A' side, the letters 'A' and 'B' in this case only refer to which side was the most popular in that particular country.

Please Mr. Postman

Please Mr. Postman /
A Hard Day's Night

Rhodesia	Parlophone	SPD 332	1964	Company	'A' Side
S Africa	Parlophone	SPD 332	1964	Company	'A' Side

Please Mr. Postman / Hold Me Tight

W Germany	Odeon	02-2741	1964	Company	'B' Side

Please Mr. Postman / Money

Japan	Odeon	OR-1102	1964	Picture	'A' Side
Japan	Apple	AR-1102	1964	Picture	'A' Side
Japan	Odeon	EAR-20245	1977	Picture	'A' Side

Please Mr. Postman / PS I Love You

France	Odeon	SO 10112	1964	Picture	'B' Side

Please Mr. Postman /
Roll Over Beethoven

Canada	Capitol	72133	1964	Company	'A' Side
Denmark	Odeon	DK 1619	1964	Picture	'B' Side
Finland	Parlophone	DPY 666	1964	Company	'A' Side
Norway	Odeon	DK 1619	1964	Picture	'B' Side
Sweden	Odeon	SD 5966	1964	Picture	'B' Side

Please Mr. Postman / Slow Down

Greece   Parlophone   GMSP 55   1964   Company   'A' Side

Please, Please Me

Please, Please Me / Ask Me Why

Australia	Parlophone	A8080	1963	Company	'A' Side
Canada	Capitol	72090	1963	Company	'A' Side
Chile	Odeon	MSOD 8432	1963	Company	'A' Side
Denmark	Parlophone	R4983	1963	Picture	'A' Side
France	Odeon	SO 10087	1964	Picture	'A' Side
France	Odeon	006-04451	1970	Company	'A' Side
India	Parlophone	45-R.4983	1963	Company	'A' Side
Ireland	Parlophone	R (I) 4983	1963	Company	'A' Side
Italy	Parlophone	QMSP 16346	1963	Picture	'A' Side
Italy	Parlophone	3C006-04451	1970	Picture	'A' Side
Japan	Odeon	OR-1024	1964	Picture	'A' Side
Japan	Apple	AR-1024	1964	Picture	'A' Side
Japan	Odeon	EAR-20222	1977	Picture	'A' Side
New Zealand	Parlophone	NZP 3142	1963	Company	'A' Side
Nigeria	Parlophone	45-R4983 NI	1963	Company	'A' Side
Norway	Parlophone	R4983	1963	Picture	'A' Side
Pakistan	Parlophone	45-R.4983	1963	Company	'A' Side
Spain	Odeon	DSOL 66.041	1963	Company	'A' Side
Spain	Odeon	1J006-04451	1970	Picture	'A' Side
Sweden	Parlophone	R4983	1963	Company	'A' Side
S Africa	Parlophone	SPD 261	1963	Company	'A' Side
Turkey	Odeon	LA 4139	1963	Picture	'A' Side
UK	Parlophone	R4983	1963	Company	'A' Side
UK	Parlophone	R4983	1983	Company	'A' Side
USA	Vee Jay	VJ 498	1963	Company	'A' Side

Please, Please Me / From Me to You

Brazil	EMI	451 3392	19?	Picture	'B' Side
Canada	Capitol	Starline 45-6063	1965	Company	'A' Side
France	Odeon	SO 10087	1963	Company	'B' Side
Greece	Parlophone	GMSP 41	1963	Company	'A' Side
Italy	Vee Jay	Bluebell VJ581	1964	Picture	'A' Side
USA	Vee Jay	VJ 581	1964	Company	'A' Side
USA	Oldies	45 OL 150	1964	Company	'A' Side
USA	Capitol	Starline 6063	1965	Company	'A' Side

Please, Please Me / I Want to Hold Your Hand

Philippines	Parlophone	PAL 60102	1963	Company	'B' Side

Please, Please Me / Love Me Do

W Germany	Odeon	22 396	1963	Company	'B' Side
Netherlands	Odeon	45-O-29469	1963	Company	'B' Side
Sweden	Odeon	SD 5937	1963	Picture	'A' Side

Rain

Rain / Paperback Writer

Australia	Parlophone	A8203	1966	Company	'B' Side
Brazil	EMI	45BT	19?	Picture	'A' Side
Canada	Capitol	5651	1966	Comp & Pic	'B' Side
Canada	Capitol	5651	1969-70	Company	'B' Side
Chile	Odeon	MSOD 8606	1966	Company	'B' Side
Denmark	Parlophone	R5452	1966	Picture	'B' Side
France	Odeon	FOS 107	1967	Company	'B' Side
Finland	Parlophone	DPY 699	1966	Company	'B' Side
Greece	Parlophone	GMSP 104	1966	Company	'B' Side
W Germany	Odeon	23 210	1966	Picture	'B' Side
India	Parlophone	45-R.5452	1966	Company	'B' Side
Ireland	Parlophone	R (I)5452	1966	Company	'B' Side
Italy	Parlophone	QMSP 16394	1966	Picture	'B' Side
Japan	Odeon	OR-1529	1966	Picture	'B' Side
Japan	Apple	AR-1529	1966	Picture	'B' Side
Japan	Odeon	EAR-20232	1977	Picture	'B' Side
Mexico	Capitol	6066	1966	Comp.& Pic	'B' Side
Netherlands	Parlophone	R5452	1966	Picture	'B' Side
NewZealand	Parlophone	NZP 3204	1966	Company	'B' Side
Nicaragua	Odeon	4O-014	1966	Picture	'B' Side
Nigeria	Parlophone	45-R-5452 NI	1966	Company	'B' Side
Norway	Parlophone	R5452	1966	Picture	'B' Side
Peru	Odeon	9573	1966	Company	'B' Side
Philippines	Parlophone	PAL 60538	1967	Company	'B' Side
Rhodesia	Parlophone	SPD 386	1966	Company	'B' Side
S Africa	Parlophone	SPD 386	1966	Company	'B' Side

Spain	Odeon	DSOL 66.073	1966	Picture	'B' Side
Sweden	Parlophone	R5452	1966	Picture	'B' Side
Switzerland	Odeon	9 23 210	1966	Picture	'B' Side
Turkey	Odeon	LA 4261	1966	Picture	'B' Side
UK	Parlophone	R5452	1966	Company	'B' Side
USA	Capitol	5651	1966	Picture	'B' Side
USA	Capitol	Target 5651	1969	Company	'B' Side
USA	Capitol J/Box	S7-18902 (Red)	1994-96	Picture	'B' Side

Real Love

Real Love / Baby's in Black

UK	Apple	R6425	1995	Picture	'A' Side
USA	Apple	NR7243 8 58544 7 7	1995	Picture	'A' Side

Revolution

Revolution / Hey Jude

Australia	Parlophone	A8493	1968	Company	'B' Side
Brazil	EMI	45BT 97	19?	Picture	'B' Side
Canada	Apple	2276	1968	Company	'B' Side
Chile	Odeon	MSOD 8769	1968	Company	'B' Side
Denmark	Apple	DP 570	1968	Picture	'B' Side
Denmark	Parlophone	DP 570	1968	Picture	'B' Side
Ecuador	Odeon	87789	1968	Company	'B' Side
France	Odeon	FOS 127	1968	Picture	'B' Side
France	Apple	FOS 127	1968	Picture	'B' Side
France	Apple	APF 504	1968	Picture	'B' Side
Finland	Parlophone	DP 570	1968	Company	'B' Side
Greece	Parlophone	GMSP 134	1968	Company	'B' Side
W Germany	Odeon	23 880	1968	Picture	'B' Side
W Germany	Apple	0 23 880	1968	Company	'B' Side
India	Parlophone	DP 570	1968	Company	'B' Side
India	Apple	DP 570	1968	Company	'B' Side
Ireland	Parlophone	DP (I) 570	1968	Company	'B' Side
Israel	Parlophone	DP 570	1968	Picture	'B' Side
Israel	Apple	DP 570	1968	Company	'B' Side
Italy	Parlophone	QMSP 16433	1968	Picture	'B' Side
Italy	Apple	QMSP 16433	1968	Picture	'B' Side
Italy	Parlophone	DP 570	1968	Picture	'B' Side
Italy	Parlophone	QMSP 16433	1968	Picture	'B' Side
Japan	Apple	AR-2121	1968	Picture	'B' Side
Japan	Odeon	OR-2121	1968	Picture	'B' Side

Japan	Odeon	EAR-20238	1977	Picture	'B' Side
Kenya	Parlophone	DP 570	1968	Company	'B' Side
Lebanon	Parlophone	MOL 19	1968	Company	'B' Side
Mexico	Capitol	6365	1968	Comp. &Pic	'B' Side
Netherlands	Parlophone	DP 570	1968	Company	'B' Side
Netherlands	Apple	DP 570	1968	Picture	'B' Side
New Zealand	Parlophone	NZP 3288	1968	Company	'B' Side
Nicaragua	Odeon	O-0302	1968	Company	'A' Side
Norway	Parlophone	DP 570	1968	Picture	'B' Side
Pakistan	Apple	DP 570	1968	Company	'B' Side
Peru	Odeon	10425	1968	Company	'B' Side
Philippines	Parlophone	PAL 60799	1968	Company	'A' Side
Portugal	Parlophone	PDP 5089	1968	Picture	'B' Side
Rhodesia	Parlophone	SPD 477	1968	Company	'B' Side
Singapore	Parlophone	DP 570	1969	Company	'B' Side
S Africa	Parlophone	SPD 477	1968	Company	B' Side
Spain	Odeon	DSOL 16.740	1968	Picture	B' Side
Sweden	Parlophone	DP 570	1968	Picture	B' Side
Turkey	Apple	R5722	1968	Company	B' Side
UK	Odeon	LA 4296	1968	Company	B' Side
UK	Apple	R5722	1968	Company	B' Side
USA	Parlophone	DP 570	1968	Company	B' Side
USA	Apple	2276	1968	Company	B' Side
USA	Capitol (J Box)	S7-17694 (Blue)	1968	Company	B' Side
Venezuela	Parlophone	7 PTM 525	1968	Company	B' Side
W Indies	Parlophone	DP 570	1968	Company	B' Side
Yugoslavia	Parlophone /Jugoton	SP8214	1968	Picture	B' Side

Revolution / Wild Honey Pie

USA	Capital	5999	1990	Company	'B' Side

Rock and Roll Music

Rock and Roll Music / Baby's in Black

Mexico	Musart	3823	1965	Company	'A' Side

Rock and Roll Music / Can't Buy Me Love

Ecuador	Odeon	87514	1965	Company	'B' Side

Rock and Roll Music / Eight Days a Week

Bolivia	Parlophone	BO-1040	1965	Picture	'B' Side
Brazil	EMI	451 3396	19?	Picture	'A' Side
Denmark	Odeon	ND 7438	1965	Picture	'A' Side
France	Odeon	SO 10128	1965	Picture	'B' Side
Finland	Parlophone	DPY 678	1965	Company	'A' Side
Norway	Odeon	ND 7438	1965	Picture	'A' Side
S Africa	Parlophone	SPD?	1965	Company	'B' Side
Turkey	Odeon	LA 4196	1965	Picture	'B' Side

Rock and Roll Music / Every Little Thing

Japan	Odeon	OR-1192	1965	Picture	'A' Side
Japan	Apple	AR-1192	1965	Picture	'A' Side
Japan	Odeon	EAR-20249	1977	Picture	'A' Side

Rock and Roll Music / Honey Don't

Australia	Parlophone	A 8143	1965	Company	'A' Side
Chile	Odeon	MSOD 8505	1965	Company	'A' Side

Rock and Roll Music / If I Fell

Sweden	Parlophone	SD 5974	1965	Picture	'A' Side

Rock and Roll Music / I'll Follow the Sun

Italy	Parlophone	QMSP 16371	1964	Picture	'A' Side

Rock and Roll Music / I'm a Loser

Belgium	Odeon	MO 20007	1966	Picture	'A' Side
France	Odeon	MO 20007	1966	Comp.& Picture	'A' Side
W Germany	Odeon	22 915	1965	Picture	'A' Side
Switzerland	Odeon	9 922 915	1965	Picture	'A' Side

Rock and Roll Music / No Reply

Greek	Parlophone	GMSP 84	1965	Picture	'A' Side
India	Parlophone	45-DPE.179	1965	Company	'A' Side
Netherlands	Parlophone	HHR 136	1965	Picture	'B' Side
Philippines	Parlophone	PAL 60283	1964	Company	'B' Side

Rock and Roll Music / Things We Said Today

Rhodesia	Parlophone	SPD 349	1964	Company	'A' Side
S Africa	Parlophone	SPD 349	1964	Company	'A' Side

Roll Over Beethoven

Roll Over Beethoven / A Hard Day's Night

Spain	Odeon	DSOL 66.057	1964	Company	'B' Side

Roll Over Beethoven / All My Loving

Mexico	Musart	3611	1964	Company	'A' Side
NewZealand	Parlophone	NZP 3158	1964	Company	'A' Side

Roll Over Beethoven / Devil in Her Heart

Philippines	Parlophone	PAL 60105	1963	Company	'A' Side

Roll Over Beethoven / Do You Want to Know a Secret

Greece	Odeon	GMSP 53	1964	Picture	'A' Side

Roll Over Beethoven / Hold Me Tight

Australia	Parlophone	A 8107	1964	Company	'A' Side
Netherlands	Odeon	O 127	1964	Company	'A' Side

Roll Over Beethoven / I Want to Be Your Man

France	Odeon	SO 10120	1964	Picture	'A' Side

Roll Over Beethoven /
I Want to Hold Your Hand

W Germany	Odeon	22 623	1963	Company	'B' Side

Roll Over Beethoven / Just Seventeen

Rhodesia	Parlophone	SPD 299	1964	Comp.&Picture	'B' Side
S Africa	Parlophone	SPD 299	1964	Comp.&Picture	'B' Side

Roll Over Beethoven / Misery

USA	Capitol	Starline 6065	1964	Company	'A' Side
USA	Capitol	Target 6065	1969	Company	'A' Side

Roll Over Beethoven / Please Mr. Postman

Canada	Capitol	72133	1963	Company	'A' Side
Denmark	Odeon	DK 1619	1964	Picture	'A' Side
Finland	Parlophone	DPY 666	1964	Company	'B' Side
Norway	Odeon	DK1619	1964	Picture	'A' Side
Sweden	Odeon	SD 5966	1964	Company	'A' Side

Roll Over Beethoven / Twist and Shout

Japan	Odeon	OR-1078	1964	Picture	'B' Side
Japan	Apple	AR-1078	1964	Picture	'B' Side
Japan	Odeon	EAR-20243	1977	Picture	'B' Side

Run for Your Life

Run for Your Life / Girl

Chile	Odeon	MSOD 8600	1966	Company	'B' Side

Run for Your Life / In My Life

Philippines	Parlophone	PAL 60471	1966	Company	'A' Side

Run for Your Life / Michelle

France	Odeon	FOS 101	1966	Company	'B' Side
Italy	Parlophone	QMSP 16389	1966	Picture	'B' Side

Sexy Sadie

Sexy Sadie / Ob-La-Di, Ob-La-Da

W Indies	Parlophone	?	1968	Company	'B' Side

Sgt Pepper

Sgt Pepper / A Day in the Life

Italy	Parlophone	PFC 7511	1967	Picture	'A' Side
Japan	Odeon	EAR-20501	1978	Picture	'A' Side
UK	Parlophone	R6022	1978	Picture	'A' Side
USA	Capitol	4612	1978	Company	'A' Side
USA	Capitol J/Box	S7-17701(Crystal)	1994-96	Company	'A' Side

She Loves You

She Loves You / I'll Get You

Australia	Parlophone	A8093	1963	Company	'A' Side
Bolivia	Parlophone	R5055	1964	Company	'A' Side
Canada	Capitol	72125	1963	Company	'A' Side
Chile	Odeon	MSOD 8421	1963	Picture	'A' Side
Denmark	Parlophone	R5055	1963	Picture	'A' Side
Ecuador	Odeon	87360	1964	Company	'A' Side
Finland	Parlophone	DPY 653	1963	Company	'A' Side
Greece	Parlophone	GMSP 42	1963	Company	'A' Side
W Germany	Odeon	22 554	1963	Company	'A' Side
India	Parlophone	45-R.5055	1963	Company	'A' Side
Ireland	Parlophone	R(I)5055	1963	Company	'A' Side
Italy	Parlophone	QMSP 16347	1963	Picture	'A' Side
Italy	Parlophone	PFC 7501	1963	Company	'A' Side
Japan	Odeon	OR-1058	1964	Picture	'A' Side
Japan	Apple	AR-1058	1964	Picture	'A' Side
Japan	Odeon	EAR-20224	1977	Picture	'A' Side
Netherlands	Parlophone	R5055	1963	Company	'A' Side
New Zealand	Parlophone	NZP 3148	1963	Company	'A' Side
Nigeria	Parlophone	45-R5055 NI	1963	Company	'A' Side
Norway	Parlophone	R5055	1963	Picture	'A' Side
Pakistan	Parlophone	R5055	1963	Company	'A' Side
Peru	Odeon	8806	1963	Company	'A' Side
Philippines	Parlophone	PAL 60106	1963	Company	'A' Side
S Africa	Parlophone	SPD 278	1963	Company	'A' Side
Sweden	Parlophone	R5055	1963	Picture	'A' Side
Turkey	Odeon	LA 4136	1963	Comp & Pict	'A' Side

UK	Parlophone	R5055	1963	Company	'A' Side
USA	Swan	4152	1963	Comp & Pict	'A' Side
USA	Capitol J/Box	S7-16788 (Red)	1994-96	Company	'A' Side

She Loves You / I Saw Her Standing There

Mexico.	Musart	3576	1964	Company	'A' Side

She Loves You / I Want to Hold Your Hand

Brazil	EMI	451 3393	19?	Picture	'A' Side
Prague	Odeon	71-3049	1964	Picture	'B' Side
Spain	Odeon	DSOL66.056	1964	Company	'A' Side

She Loves You / Twist and Shout

France	Odeon	SO 10091	1963	Company	'A' Side

She Loves You / Yesterday

Nicaragua	Odeon	01-0474	1967	Company	'B' Side

She's a Woman

She's a Woman / Anna

Peru	Odeon	9157	1964	Company	'A' Side

She's a Woman / I Feel Fine

Australia	Parlophone	A8133	1964	Company	'B' Side
Belgium	Parlophone	R5200	1964	Picture	'B' Side
Brazil	EMI	451 3395	19 ?	Picture	'A' Side
Canada	Capitol	5327	1964	Comp. & Pic	'B' Side
Canada	Capitol	Target 5327	1969-71	Company	'B' Side
Chile	Odeon	MSOD 8500	1964	Company	'B' Side
Denmark	Parlophone	R5200	1964	Picture	'B' Side
France	Odeon	SO 10125	1964	Picture	'B' Side
Finland	Parlophone	DPY674	1964	Company	'B' Side
Greece	Parlophone	GMSP 65	1964	Company	'B' Side
WGermany	Odeon	22 851	1964	Picture	'B' Side
India	Parlophone	45-R.5200	1964	Company	'B' Side
Ireland	Parlophone	R(I)5200	1964	Company	'B' Side
Israel	Parlophone	R5200	1964	Company	'B' Side
Japan	Odeon	OR-1179	1965	Picture	'B' Side
Japan	Apple	AR-1179	1965	Picture	'B' Side
Japan	Odeon	EAR-20228	1977	Picture	'B' Side
Mexico	Musart	3764	1964	Company	'B' Side
Netherlands	Parlophone	R5200	1964	Picture	'B' Side
NewZealand	Parlophone	NZP 3175	1964	Company	'B' Side
Norway	Parlophone	R5200	1964	Picture	'B' Side
Rhodesia	Parlophone	SPD 341	1964	Company	'B' Side

S Africa	Parlophone	SPD 341	1964	Company	'B' Side
Spain	Odeon	DSOL 66.046	1964	Picture	'B' Side
Sweden	Parlophone	R5200	1964	Picture	'B' Side
Turkey	Odeon	LA 4167	1964	Picture	'B' Side
UK	Parlophone	R5200	1964	Company	'B' Side
USA	Capitol	5327	1964	Picture	'B' Side
USA	Capitol	Target 5327	1969	Company	'B' Side

She's a Woman / Long Tall Sally

| France | Odeon | 2c-010-04457 | 1978 | Picture | 'B' Side |
| Italy | Parlophone | QMSP 16381 | 1965 | Picture | 'B' Side |

She's Leaving Home

She's Leaving Home / This Boy

Philippines	Parlophone	PAL 60780	1967	Company	'B' Side

Sie Liebt Dich

Sie Liebt Dich / I'll Get You

Canada	Capitol	72162	1964	Company	'A' Side

Sie Liebt Dich / Komm Gib Mir Deine Hand

Australia	Parlophone	A 8117	1964	Company	'B' Side
W Germany	Odeon	22 671	1964	Picture	'B' Side
W Germany	Odeon	1C006-04204	1969	Picture	'B' Side

Slow Down

Slow Down / Long Tall Sally

Chile	Odeon	MSOD 8486	1964	Picture	'B' Side

Slow Down / Matchbox

Canada	Capitol	5255	1964	Company	'B' Side
Canada	Capitol	Target 5255	1969-71	Company	'B' Side
Japan	Odeon	OR-1156	1964	Picture	'B' Side
Japan	Apple	AR-1156	1964	Picture	'B' Side
Japan	Odeon	EAS-17056	?	Picture	'B' Side
Philippines	Parlophone	PAL 60255	1964	Picture	'A' Side
USA	Capitol	5255	1964	Picture	'B' Side
USA	Capitol	Target 5255	1969	Company	'B' Side

Slow Down / I'm Happy Just to Dance with You

W Germany	Odeon	22 838	1964	Company	'A' Side

Slow Down / Please Mr. Postman

Greece	Parlophone	GMSP 55	1964	Picture	'B' Side

Something

Something / Come Together

Country	Label	Catalogue	Year	Type	Side
Australia	Apple	A8943	1969	Company	'A' Side
Brazil	EMI	45BT 101	19?	Picture	'A' Side
Canada	Apple	2654	1969	Company	'B' Side
Canada	Apple	2654	1969	Company	'A' Side
Chile	Apple	Apple 12	1969	Picture	'B' Side
Denmark	Apple	R5814	1969	Picture	'A' Side
Ecuador	Odeon	87862	1969	Company	'A' Side
France	Apple	2C006-04266	1969	Picture	'A' Side
Finland	Parlophone	R5814	1969	Company	'A' Side
Greece	Parlophone	GMSP 146	1969	Company	'A' Side
Guatemala	Odeon	4213	1976	Company	'A' Side
WGermany	Apple	1C006-04266	1969	Picture	'A' Side
India	Apple	45-R.5814	1969	Company	'A' Side
Ireland	Apple	R(I)5814	1969	Company	'A' Side
Israel	Apple	R5814	1969	Picture	'A' Side
Italy	Apple	QMSP 16461	1969	Picture	'A' Side
Italy	Apple	3C006-04266	1969	Picture	'A' Side
Japan	Apple	AR-2400	1969	Picture	'B' Side
Japan	Apple	EAR-20241	1977	Picture	'B' Side
Lebanon	Apple	R5814 /C006-04266MA	1969	Company	'A' Side
Mexico	Apple	6565	1969	Picture	'A' Side
Netherlands	Apple	5C006-04266	1969	Picture	'A' Side
NewZealand	Apple	NZP 3345	1969	Company	'A' Side
Norway	Apple	ND 7485	1969	Picture	'A' Side
Peru	Apple	10920	1969	Company	'B' Side

Philippines	Apple	PAL 60898	1969	Company	'B' Side
Portugal	Parlophone	8E006-04031	1969	Picture	'B' Side
Singapore	Apple	PEA-504	1969	Company	'A' Side
S Africa	Parlophone	SPD 520	1969	Company	'A' Side
Spain	Odeon	1J006-04266	1969	Picture	'A' Side
Sweden	Apple	R5814	1969	Picture	'A' Side
Turkey	Apple	LA 4313	1969	Company	'A' Side
UK	Apple	R5814	1969	Company	'A' Side
USA	Apple	2654	1969	Company	'A' Side
USA	Capitol J/Box	S7-17698 (Blue)	1994-96	Company	'A' Side
Venezuela	Odeon	OD-45-14	1969	Company	'B' Side
W Indies	Parlophone	S45-X-4699	1969	Company	'A' Side
Yugoslavia	Apple / Jugoton	SP 8334	1969	Picture	'A' Side

Strawberry Fields

Strawberry Fields / Penny Lane

Australia	Parlophone	A8243	1967	Picture	'A' Side
Brazil	EMI	45BT	19?	Picture	'A' Side
Canada	Capitol	5810	1967	Comp. & Picture	'A' Side
Canada	Capitol	5810	1969-70	Company	'A' Side
Congo	HMV	R5570	1967	Company	'A' Side
Denmark	Parlophone	R5570	1967	Picture	'A' Side
Ecuador	Odeon	87675	1967	Company	'B' Side
France	Odeon	FOS 116	1968	Comp. & Pic	'B' Side
Finland	Parlophone	R5570	1967	Company	'A' Side
Greece	Parlophone	GMSP 113	1967	Company	'A' Side
WGermany	Odeon	23 436	1967	Picture	'A' Side
India	Parlophone	45-R.5570	1967	Company	'B' Side
Ireland	Parlophone	R(I)5570	1967	Picture	'A' Side
Italy	Parlophone	QMSP 16404	1967	Picture	'A' Side
Japan	Odeon	OR-1685	1967	Picture	'A' Side
Japan	Apple	AR-1685	1967	Picture	'A' Side
Japan	Odeon	EAR-20234	1977	Picture	'A' Side
Mexico	Capitol	6160	1967	Company	'B' Side
Netherlands	Parlophone	R5570	1967	Picture	'A' Side
NewZealand	Parlophone	NZP 3224	1967	Company	'A' Side
Nicaragua	Odeon	O-0172	1967	Company	'A' Side
Nigeria	Parlophone	45-R-5570 NI	1967	Company	'A' Side
Norway	Parlophone	R5570	1967	Picture	'A' Side
Pakistan	Parlophone	R5570	1967	Company	'A' Side

Peru	Odeon	9827	1967	Company	'B' Side
Philippines	Parlophone	PAL 60617	1967	Company	'A' Side
Rhodesia	Parlophone	SPD 415	1967	Company	'A' Side
S Africa	Parlophone	SPD 415	1967	Company	'A' Side
Spain	Odeon	DSOL 66.077	1967	Picture	'A' Side
Spain	Odeon	1J006-04475	1970	Picture	'A' Side
Sweden	Parlophone	R5570	1967	Picture	'A' Side
Switzerland	Odeon	9 23 436	1967	Picture	'A' Side
Turkey	Odeon	LA 4277	1967	Company	'B' Side
UK	Parlophone	R5570	1967	Picture	'A' Side
USA	Capitol	5810	1967	Picture	'B' Side
USA	Capitol	Target 5810	1969	Company	'B' Side
USA	Capitol J/Box	S7-17697 (Red)	1994-96	Company	'B' Side
Venezuela	Odeon	167	1967	Company	'A' Side
Yugoslavia	Parlophone	SPAR58911	1967	Picture	'A' Side

This record was issued as a double 'A' side, the letters 'A' and 'B' in this case only refer to which side was the most popular in that particular country.

Taxman

Taxman / Birthday

USA   Capital J/Box   S7-17488   1994-96   Company   'A' Side

Taxman / Here, There and Everywhere

Philippines.   Parlophone   PAL60610   1967   Company   'A' Side

Tell Me What You See

Tell Me What You See / I've Just Seen a Face

Philippines   Parlophone   PAL 60393   1965   Company   'A' Side

Tell Me What You See / You Like Me Too Much

India   Parlophone   45-DPE.185   1965   Company   'B' Side

Tell Me What You See / You're Going to Lose That Girl

Japan	Odeon	OR-1426	1965	Picture	'B' Side
Japan	Apple	AR-1426	1965	Picture	'B' Side
Japan	Odeon	EAS-17063	?	Picture	'B' Side

Tell Me Why

Tell Me Why / A Hard Day's Night

France	Odeon	SO 10121	1964	Picture	'B' Side

Tell Me Why / And I Love Her

Mexico	Musart	3761	1964	Company	'B' Side

Tell Me Why / Any Time at All

Philippines	Parlophone	PAL 60219	1964	Company	'B' Side

Tell Me Why / Boys

Chile	Odeon	MSOD 8527	1965	Picture	'A' Side

Tell Me Why / If I Fell

W Germany	Odeon	22 797	1964	Company	'B' Side
Norway	Parlophone	DP 562	1964	Picture	'B' Side
UK	Parlophone	DP 562	1964	Company	'B' Side

Tell Me Why / I'll Cry Instead

India	Parlophone	45-DPE.172	1965	Company	'A' Side

Tell Me Why /
I'm Happy Just to Dance with You

Japan	Odeon	OR-1172	1965		Picture	'B' Side
Japan	Apple	AR-1172	1965		Picture	'B' Side
Japan	Odeon	EAS-17057	?		Picture	'B' Side

Tell Me Why / I Should Have Known Better

Denmark	Odeon	DK 1624	1964		Picture	'B' Side
Greece	Parlophone	GMSP 57	1964		Picture	'B' Side
Italy	Odeon	QMSP 16367	1964		Picture	'B' Side
Netherlands	Parlophone	HHR 128	1964		Picture	'B' Side

Thank You Girl

Thank You Girl / All My Loving

| Italy | Parlophone | QMSP 16364 | 1964 | Picture | 'A' Side |

Thank You Girl / Can't Buy Me Love

| Greece | Parlophone | GMSP 47 | 1964 | Picture | 'B' Side |

Thank You Girl / Do You Want to Know a Secret

Canada	Capitol	72159	1964	Company	'B' Side
Italy.	Bluebell V/J	VJ 587	1964	Picture	'A' Side
Japan	Odeon	OR-1093	1964	Picture	'B' Side
Japan	Apple	AR-1093	1964	Picture	'B' Side
Japan	Odeon	EAS-17055	?	Picture	'B' Side
USA	Capitol	Starline 6064	1965	Company	'B' Side
USA	Vee Jay	VJ 587	1964	Picture	'A' Side
USA	oldies	45 OL 149	1964	Company	'B' Side

Thank You Girl / From Me to You

Australia	Parlophone	A 8083	1963	Company	'B' Side
Canada	Capitol	72101	1963	Company	'B' Side
Chile	Odeon	MSOD 8440	1963	Company	'B' Side
Denmark	Parlophone	R5015	1963	Picture	'B' Side
Finland	Parlophone	DPY 652	1963	company	'B' Side
W Germany	Odeon	22 416	1963	Company	'B' Side
India	Parlophone	45-R.5015	1963	Company	'B' Side

Ireland	Parlophone	R(I)5015	1963	Company	'B' Side
Netherlands	Odeon	45-O-29470	1963	Company	'B' Side
New Zealand	Parlophone	NZP 3143	1963	Company	'B' Side
Norway	Parlophone	R5015	1963	Picture	'B' Side
Peru	Odeon	8977	1964	Company	'B' Side
Philippines	Parlophone	PAL 60107	1963	Company	'B' Side
Rhodesia	Parlophone	SPD 267	1963	Company	'B' Side
S Africa	Parlophone	SPD 267	1963	Company	'B' Side
Turkey	Odeon	LA4137	1963	Picture	'B' Side
UK	Parlophone	R5051	1963	Company	'B' Side
USA	Vee Jay	VJ 522	1963	Company	'B' Side

The Ballad of John and Yoko

The Ballad of John and Yoko / Old Brown Shoe

Australia	Apple	A8793	1969	Company	'A' Side
Brazil	EMI	45BT 100	19?	Picture	'A' Side
Canada	Apple	2531	1969	Comp. & Pic	'A' Side
Chile	Apple	Apple 9	1969	Company	'A' Side
Denmark	Apple	R5786	1969	Picture	'A' Side
Ecuador	Odeon	87828	1969	Company	'A' Side
France	Apple	2C006-04108	1969	Picture	'A' Side
Finland	Parlophone	R5786	1969	Company	'A' Side
Greece	Parlophone	GMSP 141	1969	Company	'A' Side
W Germany	Apple	1C006-04108	1969	Picture	'A' Side
India	Apple	45-R.5786	1969	Company	'A' Side
Ireland	Apple	R(I)5786	1969	Company	'A' Side
Israel	Apple	R5786	1969	Picture	'A' Side
Italy	Apple	QMSP 16456	1969	Picture	'A' Side
Italy	Apple	3C006-04108	1969	Picture	'A' Side
Japan	Apple	AR-2301	1969	Picture	'A' Side
Japan	Apple	EAR-20240	1977	Picture	'A' Side
Kenya	Parlophone	R5786	1969	Company	'A' Side
Lebanon	Apple	R5786	1969	Company	'A' Side
Malaysia	Apple	R5786	1969	Company	'A' Side
Mexico	Apple	6510	1969	Picture	'A' Side
Netherlands	Apple	5C006-04108	1969	Picture	'A' Side
NewZealand	Apple	NZP 3329	1969	Company	'A' Side
Norway	Apple	R5786	1969	Picture	'A' Side
Peru	Apple	10717	1969	Company	'A' Side
Philippines	Apple	PAL 60871	1969	Company	'A' Side

Portugal	Parlophone	PDP 5092	1969	Picture	'A' Side
Singapore	Apple	R5786	1969	Company	'A' Side
S Africa	Parlophone	SPD 516	1969	Company	'A' Side
Spain	Odeon	1J006-04108	1969	Picture	'A' Side
Sweden	Apple	R5786	1969	Picture	'A' Side
Turkey	Apple	LA 4310	1969	Company	'A' Side
UK	Apple	R5786	1969	Company	'A' Side
USA	Apple	2531	1969	Picture	'A' Side
Venezuela	Odeon	OD-45-1A	1969	Company	'A' Side
Yugoslavia	Apple / Jugoton	SAP 8304	1969	Company	'A' Side

The Inner Light

The Inner Light / Lady Madonna

Australia	Parlophone	A8293	1968	Company	'B' Side
Belgium	Parlophone	R5675	1968	Picture	'B' Side
Brazil	EMI	45BT 96	19?	Picture	'B' Side
Canada	Capitol	2138	1968	Comp & Pic	'B' Side
Chile	Odeon	MSOD 8725	1968	Picture	'B' Side
Denmark	Parlophone	R5675	1968	Picture	'B' Side
Ecuador	Odeon	87754	1968	Company	'B' Side
France	Odeon	FO 111	1968	Picture	'B' Side
Finland	Parlophone	R5675	1968	Company	'B' Side
Greece	Parlophone	GMSP 129	1968	Company	'B' Side
W Germany	Odeon	23 733	1968	Picture	'B' Side
India	Parlophone	45-R.5675	1968	Company	'B' Side
Ireland	Parlophone	R(I)5675	1968	Company	'B' Side
Israel	Parlophone	R5675	1968	Picture	'B' Side
Italy	Parlophone	QMSP 16423	1968	Picture	'B' Side
Italy	Parlophone	R5675	1968	Company	'B' Side
Japan	Odeon	OR-1902	1968	Picture	'B' Side
Japan	Apple	AR-1902	1968	Picture	'B' Side
Japan	Odeon	EAR-20237	1977	Picture	'B' Side
Kenya	Parlophone	R5675	1968	Company	'A' Side
Lebanon	Parlophone	MOL.13	1968	Company	'B' Side
Mexico	Capitol	6310	1968	Picture	'B' Side
Netherlands	Parlophone	R5675	1968	Picture	'B' Side
New Zealand	Parlophone	NZP 3265	1968	Company	'B' Side

Norway	Parlophone	R5675	1968	Picture	'B' Side
Pakistan	Parlophone	R5675	1968	Company	'B' Side
Peru	Odeon	10274	1968	Company	'B' Side
Philippines	Parlophone	PAL 60752	1968	Company	'B' Side
Portugal	Parlophone	PDP 5085	1968	Company	'B' Side
Rhodesia	Parlophone	SPD 386	1966	Company	'B' Side
S Africa	Parlophone	SPD 456	1968	Company	'B' Side
Singapore	Parlophone	R5675	1968	Company	'B' Side
Spain	Odeon	DSOL 66.740	1968	Picture	'B' Side
Spain	Odeon	1J006-04478	1970	Picture	'B' Side
Sweden	Parlophone	R5675	1968	Picture	'B' Side
Turkey	Odeon	LA 4286	1968	Company	'B' Side
UK	Parlophone	R5675	1968	Company	'B' Side
USA	Capitol	2138	1968	Picture	'B' Side
USA	Capitol	Target 2138	1969	Company	'B' Side
Venezuela	Parlophone	7PMT 524	1968	Company	'B' Side
W Indies	Parlophone	StatesideR5675	1968	Company	'B' Side
Yugoslavia	Parl/Jugoton	SPP8175	1968	Picture	'B' Side

The Long and Winding Road

The Long and Winding Road / For You Blue

Australia	Apple	A9163	1970	Company	'A' Side
Brazil	EMI	45BT 103	19?	Picture	'A' Side
Canada	Apple	2832	1970	Comp. & Pict	'A' Side
Chile	Apple	Apple 18	1970	Company	'A' Side
Denmark	Apple	6C006-04514	1970	Picture	'A' Side
France	Apple	2C006-04514	1970	Picture	'A' Side
Finland	Apple	5E006-04514	1970	Company	'A' Side
Greece	Parlophone	GMSP 149	1970	Company	'A' Side
W Germany	Apple	1C006-04514	1970	Picture	'A' Side
Italy	Apple	3C006-04514	1970	Picture	'A' Side
Japan	Apple	AR-2611	1970	Picture	'A' Side
Japan	Apple	EAR-20253	1977	Picture	'A' Side
Lebanon	Apple	MOL 42	1970	Company	'A' Side
Mexico	Apple	6680	1970	Company	'A' Side
Netherlands	Apple	2832	1970	Picture	'A' Side
New Zealand	Apple	NZP 3371`	1970	Company	'A' Side
Norway	Apple	7E006-04514	1970	Picture	'A' Side
Philippines	Apple	PAL 60938	1970	Company	'A' Side
Singapore	Apple	PEA-505	1970	Company	'A' Side
Spain	Odeon	1J006-04514	1970	Picture	'A' Side
Sweden	Apple	4E006-04514	1970	Picture	'A' Side
Turkey	Odeon	LA 4321	1970	Company	'A' Side
USA	Apple	2832	1970	Picture	'A' Side
USA	Capitol	S7-18898	1994-	Company	'A' Side
	J/Box	(Blue)	96		

The Long and Winding Road / I, Me, Mine

Venezuela	Apple	AP 1804	1970	Company	'A' Side

The Night Before

The Night Before / Another Girl

Japan	Odeon	OR-1430	1965	Picture	'A' Side
Japan	Apple	AR-1430	1965	Picture	'A' Side
Japan	Odeon	EAS-17064	?	Picture	'A' Side

The Night Before / Dizzy Miss Lizzy

India	Parlophone	45-DPE.183	1965	Company	'B' Side

The Night Before / Yesterday

Italy	Parlophone	QMSP163 8	1965	Picture	'B' Side

The Night Before / You Like Me Too Much

Philippines	Parlophone	PAL 60392	1965	Company	'B' Side

The Night Before / You've Got to Hide Your Love Away

Greece	Parlophone	GMSP 96	1965	Company	'A' Side

The Word

The Word / Michelle

| Philippines | Parlophone | PAL 60557 | 1967 | | Company | 'B' Side |

The Word / Nowhere Man

| France | Odeon | FOS 108 | 1967 | | Company | 'B' Side |

There's a Place

There's a Place / Anna

Chile	Odeon	MSOD8533	1965	Picture	'A' Side

There's a Place / Ask Me Why

Philippines	Parlophone	PAL60274	1964	Company	'B' Side

There's a Place / Twist and Shout

Canada	Capitol	72146	1964	Company	'B' Side
Canada	Capitol	*Starline* 45-6061	1965	Company	'B' Side
Canada	Capitol	72146	1969-71	Company	'B' Side
Italy	Bluebell	*Tollie* T9001	1964	Picture	'B' Side
USA	Tollie	9001	1964	Company	'B' Side
USA	Oldies	45 OL 152	1964	Company	'B' Side
USA	Capitol	Starline 6061	1965	Company	'B' Side
USA	Capitol J/Box	S7-17699 (Pink)	1994-96	Company	'B' Side

Things We Said Today

Things We Said Today / A Hard Day's Night

Australia	Parlophone	A 8123	1964	Company	'B' Side
Austria	Parlophone	O 28521	1964	Picture	'B' Side
Belgium	Parlophone	R5160	1964	Company	'B' Side
Denmark	Parlophone	R5160	1964	Picture	'B' Side
Finland	Parlophone	DPY 668	1964	Company	'B' Side
W Germany	Odeon	22 760	1964	Company	'B' Side
Guatemala	Odeon	4261	1976	Company	'B' Side
India	Parlophone	45-R.5160	1964	Picture	'B' Side
Ireland	Parlophone	R(I)5160	1964	Picture	'B' Side
Israel	Parlophone	R5160	1964	Company	'B' Side
Italy	Parlophone	QSMP 16363	1964	Picture	'B' Side
Japan	Apple	AR-1119	1964	Picture	'B' Side
Japan	Odeon	OR-1119	1964	Picture	'B' Side
Japan	Odeon	EAR-20227	1977	Picture	'B' Side
Mexico	Musart	3669	1964	Company	'B' Side
Netherlands	Parlophone	R5160	1964	Picture	'B' Side
NewZealand	Parlophone	NZP 3167	1964	Company	'B' Side
Norway	Parlophone	R5160	1964	Picture	'B' Side
Philippines	Parlophone	PAL 60197	1964	Company	'B' Side
Sweden	Parlophone	R5160	1964	Picture	'B' Side
Turkey	Odeon	LA 4153	1964	Picture	'A' Side
UK	Parlophone	R5160	1964	Company	'B' Side
USA	Capitol J/Box	S717692(White)	1994-96	Company	'B' Side

Things We Said Today /
I'm Happy Just to Dance with You

France	Odeon	SO 10122	1965	Picture	'B' Side

Things We Said Today / Rock and Roll Music

Rhodesia	Parlophone	SPD 349	1964	Company	'B' Side
S Africa	Parlophone	SPD 349	1964	Company	'B' Side

This Boy

This Boy / All My Loving

Canada	Capitol	72144	1964	Company	'B' Side
Canada	Capitol	72144	1969-71	Company	'B' Side

This Boy / From Me to You

Mexico	Musart	3596	1964	Company	'B' Side

This Boy / I'll Get You

France	Odeon	SO 10117	1964	Picture	'A' Side

This Boy / I Want to Hold Your Hand

Australia	Parlophone	A 8103	1963	Company	'B' Side
Chile	Odeon	MSOD 8420	1963	Picture	'B' Side
Denmark	Parlophone	R5084	1963	Picture	'B' Side
Ecuador	Odeon	87361	1964	Company	'B' Side
Finland	Parlophone	DPY 655	1964	Company	'B' Side
India	Parlophone	45-R5084	1963	Company	'B' Side
Ireland	Parlophone	R(I)5084	1963	Company	'B' Side
Japan	Odeon	OR-1041	1963	Picture	'B' Side
Japan	Apple	AR-1041	1963	Picture	'B' Side
Japan	Odeon	EAR-20225	1977	Picture	'B' Side
Netherlands	Parlophone	R5084	1963	Company	'B' Side
New Zealand	Parlophone	NZP 3152	1963	Company	'B' Side
Nigeria	Parlophone	45-R5084 NI	1963	Company	'B' Side
Norway	Parlophone	R5084	1963	Picture	'B' Side

Pakistan	Parlophone	R5084	1964	Company	'B' Side
Peru	Odeon	8856	1963	Company	'B' Side
Sweden	Parlophone	R5084	1963	Picture	'B' Side
S Africa	Parlophone	SPD 293	1963	Company	'B' Side
Turkey	Odeon	LA 4138	1963	Picture	'B' Side
UK	Parlophone	R5084	1963	Company	'B' Side
USA	Capitol	S7-17689	1994-	Company	'B' Side
	J/Box	(Crystal)	96		

This Boy / She's Leaving Home

Philippines	Parlophone	PAL 60780	1967	Company	'A' Side

This Boy / Ticket to Ride

Brazil	EMI	451 3397	19?	Picture	'A' Side
Prague	Odeon	71-3134	1965	Picture	'B' Side

Ticket to Ride

Ticket to Ride / Eight Days a Week

Peru	Odeon	9247	1965	Company	'A' Side

Ticket to Ride / I Don't Want to Spoil the Party

France	Odeon	SO 10129	1965	Picture	'A' Side

Ticket to Ride / This Boy

Brazil	EMI	451 3397	19?	Picture	'B' Side
Prague	Odeon	71-3134	1965	Picture	'A' Side

Ticket to Ride / Yes It Is

Australia	Parlophone	A8153	1965	Company	'A' Side
Austria	Parlophone	O 28523	1965	Picture	'A' Side
Belgium	Parlophone	R5265	1965	Picture	'A' Side
Canada	Capitol	5407	1965	Comp &Pict	'A' Side
Canada	Capitol	Target 5407	1969-71	Company	'A' Side
Chile	Odeon	MSOD 8511	1965	Company	'A' Side
Denmark	Parlophone	R5265	1965	Picture	'A' Side
Finland	Parlophone	DPY 680	1965	Company	'A' Side
Greece	Parlophone	GMSP 86	1965	Company	'A' Side
W Germany	Odeon	22 950	1965	Picture	'A' Side
India	Parlophone	45-R.5265	1965	Company	'A' Side
Ireland	Parlophone	R(I)5265	1965	Company	'A' Side
Israel	Parlophone	R5265	1965	Company	'A' Side

Italy	Parlophone	QMSP 16378	1965	Picture	'A' Side
Japan	Odeon	OR-1261	1965	Picture	'A' Side
Japan	Apple	AR-1261	1965	Picture	'A' Side
Japan	Odeon	EAR-20229	1977	Picture	'A' Side
Netherlands	Parlophone	R5265	1965	Company	'A' Side
New Zealand	Parlophone	NZP 3182	1965	Company	'A' Side
Norway	Parlophone	R5265	1965	Picture	'A' Side
Philippines	Parlophone	PAL 60323	1965	Company	'A' Side
Rhodesia	Parlophone	SPD 352	1965	Company	'A' Side
S Africa	Parlophone	SPD 352	1965	Company	'A' Side
Spain	Odeon	DSOL 66.064	1965	Picture	'A' Side
Sweden	Parlophone	R5265	1965	Picture	'A' Side
Switzerland	Parlophone	9 922 950	1965	Picture	'A' Side
Turkey	Odeon	LA 4197	1965	Picture	'A' Side
UK	Parlophone	R5265	1965	Company	'A' Side
USA	Capitol	5407	1965	Picture	'A' Side
USA	Capitol	Target 5407	1969	Company	'A' Side

Till There Was You

Till There Was You / I Saw Her Standing There

France	Odeon	SO 10107	1964	Picture	'B' Side
France	Odeon	MO 20006	1966	Company	'B' Side

Till There Was You / I Want to Be Your Man

Philippines	Parlophone	PAL 60270	1964	Company	'B' Side

Till There Was You / PS I Love You

France	Odeon	SO 10104	1963	Picture	'B' Side

Twist and Shout

Twist and Shout / Back in the USSR

Brazil	EMI	451 3402	19?	Picture	'B' Side
Chile	Odeon	1181	1974	Company	'B' Side
Guatemala	Odeon	4218	1976	Company	'B' side
Philippines	Parlophone	PAL 61154	1971	Company	'B' Side
UK	Parlophone	R6016	1976	Picture	'B' Side

Twist and Shout / Boys

Denmark	Parlophone	SD 5946	1963	Picture	'A' Side
Finland	Parlophone	DPY 654	1963	Company	'A' Side
W Germany	Odeon	22 581	1963	Company	'A' Side
New Zealand	Parlophone	NZP 3160	1964	Company	'A' Side
Norway.	Parlophone	R5946	1963	Picture	'A' Side
Norway.	Parlophone	SD 5946	1963	Picture	'A' Side
Spain.	Odeon	DSOL 66.055	1964	Picture	'A' Side
Sweden	Odeon	SD 5946	1963	Picture	'A' Side
UK	Parlophone	R6016	1976	Picture	'B' Side

Twist and Shout / Do You Want to Know a Secret

Chile	Odeon	MSOD 8454	1963	Company	'A' Side
Mexico	Musart	3615	1964	Company	'A' Side
Netherlands	Odeon	HHR 125	1963	Company	'A' Side
Philippines	Parlophone	PAL 60103	1963	Company	'A' Side
Rhodesia	Parlophone	SPD 283	1963	Company	'A' Side

S Africa	Parlophone	SPD 283	1963	Company	'A' Side

Twist and Shout / Love Me Do

Ecuador	Odeon	87386	1964	Company	'B' Side
Greece	Parlophone	GMSP 43	1964	Picture	'B' Side
Greece	Parlophone	GMSP 44	1964	Picture	'A' Side

Twist and Shout / I Saw Her Standing There

Peru	Odeon	8920	1964	Company	'B' Side

Twist and Shout / Misery

Italy	Parlophone	QMSP16352	1964	Picture	'A' Side
Italy	Parlophone	PFC7503	1966	Company	'A' Side

Twist and Shout / PS I Love You

Turkey	Odeon	LA 4143	1964	Picture	'A' Side

Twist and Shout / Roll Over Beethoven

Japan	Odeon	OR-1078	1964	Picture	'A' Side
Japan	Apple	AR-1078	1964	Picture	'A' Side
Japan	Odeon	EAR-20243	1977	Picture	'A' Side

Twist and Shout / She Loves You

France	Odeon	SO 10091	1963	Company	'B' Side

Twist and Shout / There's a Place

Italy	Bluebell	Tollie T9001	1964	Picture	'A' Side
Canada	Capitol	72146	1964	Company	'A' Side
Canada	Capitol	Starline 45-6061	1965	Company	'A' Side
Canada	Capitol	72146	1969-71	Company	'A' Side
USA	Tollie	9001	1964	Company	'A' Side
USA	Oldies	45 OL 152	1964	Company	'A' Side
USA	Capitol	Starline 6061	1965	Company	'A' Side
USA	Capitol J/Box	S7-17699 (Pink)	1994-96	Company	'A' Side

Two of Us

Two of Us / Across the Universe

Philippines	Parlophone	PAL 60945	1970	Company	'B' Side
USA	Capitol J/Box	S718891(Crystal)	1994-96	Company	'B' Side

We Can Work It Out

We Can Work It Out / Day Tripper

Australia	Parlophone	A8183	1965	Company	'A' Side
Belgium	Parlophone	R5389	1965	Picture	'A' Side
Brazil	Odeon	31c00604470	1970	Company	'B' Side
Brazil	EMI	45BT 89	19?	Picture	'B' Side
Canada	Capitol	5555	1965	Company	'B' Side
Canada	Capitol	Target 5555	1969-71	Comp. & Pic	'B' Side
Chile	Odeon	MSOD 8560	1965	Company	'A' Side
Denmark	Parlophone	R5389	1965	Picture	'A' Side
France	Odeon	SO 10133	1965	Picture	'A' Side
Finland	Parlophone	DPY 689	1965	Company	'A' Side
Greece	Parlophone	GMSP 101	1965	Company	'A' Side
W Germany	Odeon	23 122	1965	Picture	'A' Side
India	Parlophone	45-R.5389	1965	Company	'A' Side
Ireland	Parlophone	R (I)5389	1965	Company	'A' Side
Israel	Parlophone	R5389	1965	Company	'A' Side
Italy	Parlophone	QMSP 16388	1966	Picture	'A' Side
Italy	Apple	3C006-04108	1969	Picture	'A' Side
Japan	Apple	AR-1445	1966	Picture	'A' Side
Japan	Odeon	OR-1445	1966	Picture	'A' Side
Japan	Odeon	EAR-20231	1977	Picture	'A' Side
Mexico	Capitol	6025	1965	Comp. & Pic	'B' Side
Netherlands	Parlophone	R5389	1965	Picture	'A' Side
New Zealand	Parlophone	NZP 3194	1965	Company	'A' Side
Nigeria	Parlophone	45-R-5389 NI	1965	Company	'A' Side
Norway	Parlophone	R5389	1965	Picture	'A' Side
Peru	Capitol	5555	1965	Company	'A' Side

Peru	Odeon	9448	1965	Company	'A' Side
Philippines	Parlophone	PAL 60436	1965	Company	'A' Side
Portugal	Parlophone	PDP 5081	1966	Company	'A' Side
Rhodesia	Parlophone	SPD 372	1965	Company	'A' Side
S Africa	Parlophone	SPD 372	1965	Company	'A' Side
Sweden	Parlophone	R5389	1965	Picture	'A' Side
Switzerland	Odeon	9 23 122	1965	Picture	'A' Side
Turkey	Odeon	LA 4246	1966	Picture	'A' Side
UK	Parlophone	R5389	1965	Company	'A' Side
USA	Capitol	5555	1965	Picture	'A' Side
USA	Capitol	Starline 5555	1969	Company	'A' Side
USA	Capitol	Target 5555	1969	Company	'A' Side
Venezuela	Odeon	70 MT 117	1965	Company	'A' Side

This record was issued as a double 'A' side, the letters 'A' and 'B' in this case only refer to which side was the most popular in that particular country.

What Goes On

What Goes On / I'm Looking Through You

India	Parlophone	45-DPE.193	1970	Company	'B' Side
Philippines	Parlophone	PAL 60472	1967	Company	'B' Side
S Africa	Parlophone	SDP 390	1966	Company	'A' Side

What Goes On / Nowhere Man

Canada	Capitol	5587	1966	Comp &Pic	'B' Side
W Germany	Odeon	23 171	1966	Picture	'B' Side
Japan	Odeon	OR-1510	1966	Picture	'B' Side
Japan	Apple	AR-1510	1966	Picture	'B' Side
Japan	Odeon	EAS-17065	?	Picture	'B' Side
Switzerland	Odeon	9 23 171	1966	Picture	'B' Side
USA	Capitol	5587	1966	Picture	'B' Side
USA	Capitol	Target 5586	1969	Company	'B' Side
USA	Capitol J/Box	S7-18894 (Green)	1994-96	Company	'B' Side

What Goes On / I'm Looking Through You

India	Parlophone	45-DPE.193	1970	Company	'B' Side
Philippines	Parlophone	PAL 60472	1967	Company	'B' Side
S Africa	Parlophone	SDP 390	1966	Company	'A' Side

What You're Doing

What You're Doing / Everybody's Trying to Be My Baby

| Greece | Parlophone | GMSP 83 | 1965 | Picture | 'B' Side |
| Philippines | Parlophone | PAL 60339 | 1965 | Picture | 'A' Side |

What You're Doing / Mr. Moonlight

Japan	Odeon	OR-1193	1965	Picture	'A' Side
Japan	Apple	AR-1193	1965	Picture	'A' Side
Japan	Odeon	EAS-17059	?	Picture	'A' Side

What You're Doing / No Reply

| Peru | Odeon | 9221 | 1965 | Company | 'A' Side |

When I'm Sixty-Four

When I'm Sixty-Four / Lucy in the Sky with Diamonds

| USA | CapitolJ/Box | S7-18896 (Red) | 1994-96 | Company | 'B' Side |

While My Guitar Gently Weeps

While My Guitar Gently Weeps / Blackbird

USA	Capitol J/Box	S7-18892 (Blue)	1994-96	Company	'A' Side

While My Guitar Gently Weeps / Ob-La-De, Ob-La-Da

Australia	Apple	A 8693	1969	Company	'B' Side
Brazil	EMI	45BT 98	19?	Picture	'B' Side
Chile	Apple	Apple 5	1968	Company	'B' Side
Ecuador	Odeon	87839	1969	Company	'B' Side
France	Odeon	FO 148	1969	Picture	'B' Side
W Germany	Apple	24004	1968	Company	'B' Side
Greece	Parlophone	GMSP 137	1968	Company	'B' Side
India	Parlophone	45-DPE.192	1968	Company	'B' Side
Israel	Apple	FO 148	1968	Picture	'B' Side
Japan	Apple	AR-2207	1969	Picture	'B' Side
Japan	Apple	EAR-20251	1977	Picture	'B' Side
Lebanon	Parlophone	MOL 29	1969	Company	'B' Side
New Zealand	Apple	NZP 3318	1969	Company	'B' Side
Netherlands	Apple	HHR 142	1969	Picture	'B' Side
Philippines	Apple	PAL 60838	1968	Company	'B' Side
Spain	Odeon	OSL-203	1969	Picture	'B' Side
Spain	Odeon	J006-04690	1970	Picture	'B' Side
Turkey	Apple	LA 4302	1968	Company	'B' Side

Why Don't We Do It in the Road

Why Don't We Do It in the Road /
Ob-La-De, Ob-La-Da

Nicaragua	Odeon	O-0363	1963	Company	'B' Side

Words of Love

Words of Love /
I Don't Want to Spoil the Party

Philippines	Parlophone	PAL 60338	1965	Company	'B' Side

Words of Love / I'll Follow the Sun

India	Parlophone	45-DPE.180	1965	Company	'B' Side
Kenya	Columbia	45-DPE 180	1965	Company	'B' Side

Words of Love / Matchbox

Rhodesia	Parlophone	SPD 356	1965	Company	'A' Side
S Africa	Parlophone	SPD 356	1965	Company	'A' Side

Yellow Submarine

Yellow Submarine / Eleanor Rigby

Australia	Parlophone	A8213	1966	Company	'A' Side
Belgium	Parlophone	R5493	1966	Company	'A' Side
Brazil	EMI	45BT 92	19?	Company	'A' Side
Canada	Capitol	5715	1966	Comp. &Pic	'A' Side
Canada	Capitol	5715	1969/70	Company	'A' Side
Chile	Odeon	MSOD 8616	1966	Company	'A' Side
Denmark	Parlophone	R5493	1966	Picture	'A' Side
Finland	Parlophone	DPY 703	1966	Company	'A' Side
France	Odeon	FOS 110	1967	Company	'A' Side
Greece	Parlophone	GMSP 109	1966	Company	'A' Side
Guatemala	Odeon	4206	1976	Company	'A' Side
WGermany	Odeon	23 280	1966	Picture	'A' Side
India	Parlophone	45-R.5493	1966	Company	'B' Side
Ireland	Parlophone	R(I)5493	1966	Company	'A' Side
Italy	Parlophone	QMSP 16397	1966	Picture	'A' Side
Japan	Apple	AR-1578	1966	Picture	'A' Side
Japan	Odeon	OR-1578	1966	Picture	'A' Side
Japan	Apple	EAR-20233	1977	Picture	'A' Side
Mexico	Capitol	6087	1966	Comp. &Pic	'A' Side
Netherlands	Parlophone	R5493	1966	Picture	'A' Side
NewZealand	Parlophone	NZP 3212	1966	Company	'A' Side
Nicaragua	Capitol	C-1104 (18396)	1967	Company	'A' Side
Norway	Parlophone	R5493	1966	Picture	'A' Side
Peru	Odeon	9635	1966	Company	'A' Side
Philippines	Parlophone	PAL 60549	1967	Company	'B' Side
Rhodesia	Parlophone	SPD 393	1966	Company	'B' Side

S Africa	Parlophone	SPD 393	1966	Company	'B' Side
Sweden	Parlophone	R5493	1966	Picture	'A' Side
Switzerland	Odeon	9 23 280	1966	Picture	'A' Side
Turkey	Odeon	LA 4263	1966	Company	'A' Side
UK	Parlophone	R5493	1966	Company	'A' Side
USA	Capitol	5715	1966	Picture	'A' Side
USA	Capitol	Target 5715	1969	Company	'A' Side
USA	Capitol J/Box	S7-17696 (Yellow)	1994-96	Company	'A' Side

Yes It Is

Yes It Is / Ticket to Ride

Australia	Parlophone	A8153	1965	Company	'B' Side
Austria	Parlophone	O 28523	1965	Picture	'B' Side
Belgium	Parlophone	R5265	1965	Picture	'B' Side
Canada	Capitol	5407	1965	Comp & Pict	'B' Side
Canada	Capitol	Target 5407	1969-71	Company	'B' Side
Chile	Odeon	MSOD 8511	1965	Company	'B' Side
Denmark	Parlophone	R5265	1965	Picture	'B' Side
Finland	Parlophone	DPY 680	1965	Company	'B' Side
Greece	Parlophone	GMSP 86	1965	Company	'B' Side
W Germany	Odeon	22 950	1965	Picture	'B' Side
India	Parlophone	45-R.5265	1965	Company	'B' Side
Ireland	Parlophone	R (I)5265	1965	Company	'B' Side
Israel	Parlophone	R5265	1965	Company	'B' Side
Italy	Parlophone	QMSP 16378	1965	Picture	'B' Side
Japan	Odeon	OR-1261	1965	Picture	'B' Side
Japan	Apple	AR-1261	1965	Picture	'B' Side
Japan	Odeon	EAR-20229	1977	Picture	'B' Side

Netherlands	Parlophone	R5265	1965	Company	'B' Side
New Zealand	Parlophone	NZP 3182	1965	Company	'B' Side
Norway	Parlophone	R5265	1965	Picture	'B' Side
Philippines	Parlophone	PAL 60323	1965	Company	'B' Side
Rhodesia	Parlophone	SPD 352	1965	Company	'B' Side
S Africa	Parlophone	SPD 352	1965	Company	'B' Side
Spain	Odeon	DSOL 66.064	1965	Picture	'B' Side
Sweden	Parlophone	R5265	1965	Picture	'B' Side
Switzerland	Parlophone	9 922 950	1965	Picture	'B' Side
Turkey	Odeon	LA 4197	1965	Picture	'B' Side
UK	Parlophone	R5265	1965	Company	'B' Side
USA	Capitol	5407	1965	Picture	'B' Side
USA	Capitol	Target 5407	1969	Company	'B' Side

Yesterday

Yesterday / Act Naturally

Australia	Parlophone	A 8173	1965	Company	'A' Side
Canada	Capitol	5498	1965	Company and Pic	'A' Side
Canada	Capitol	5498	1969	Company	'A' Side
Chile	Odeon	MSOD 8545	1965	Company	'A' Side
Denmark	Odeon	DK 1635	1965	Picture	'A' Side
W Germany	Odeon	23 031	1965	Picture	'B' Side
India	Parlophone	45-DPE.184	1965	Company	'A' Side
Japan	Apple	AR-1437	1965	Picture	'B' Side
Japan	Odeon	OR-1437	1965	Picture	'B' Side
Japan	Apple	EAR-20030	1976	Picture	'B' Side
New Zealand	Parlophone	NZP 3192	1965	Company	'A' Side
Norway	Odeon	ND 7442	1965	Picture	'A' Side
Peru	Odeon	9415	1965	Company	'A' Side
Switzerland	Odeon	9 23 031	1965	Picture	'B' Side
USA	Capitol	5498	1965	Picture	'A' Side
USA	Capitol	Target 5498	1969	Company	'A' Side
USA	Capitol J/Box	S7-18901(Pink)	1994-96	Company	'A' Side

Yesterday / Dizzy Miss Lizzy

Belgium	Parlophone	DP 563	1965	Picture	'A' Side
Congo	HMV	DP 563	1965	Company	'A' Side
Finland	Parlophone	DPY 686	1965	Company	'A' Side
Greece	Parlophone	GMSP 95	1965	Company	'A' Side

257

Mexico	Capitol	6020	1965	Company	'A' Side
Netherlands	Parlophone	HHR 138	1965	Picture	'B' Side
Sweden	Parlophone	SD 5983	1965	Picture	'B' Side
Turkey	Odeon	LA 4232	1965	Picture	'A' Side
UK	Parlophone	DP 563	1965	Company	'A' Side

Yesterday / I Should Have Known Better

Czech	Supraphon	1 43 2026	1976	Picture	'A' Side
Guatemala	Odeon	4176	1976	Company	'A' Side
Japan	Apple	EAR-20030	1976	Picture	'A' Side
Portugal	Parlophone	8E-006-06103	1965	Company	'A' Side
S Africa	Parlophone	SPD?	1965	Company	'A' Side
UK	Parlophone	R6013	1976	Picture	'A' Side
Yugoslavia	Parlophone	88895	1976	Picture	'A' Side

Yesterday / Michelle

Brazil	EMI	45BT 91	19?	Picture	'B' Side

Yesterday / She Loves You

Nicaragua	Odeon	01-0474	1967	Picture	'A' Side

Yesterday / The Night Before

French	Odeon	C006 04454	1967	Picture	'A' Side
Italy	Parlophone	QMSP 16384	1965	Picture	'A' Side

Yesterday / You've Got to Hide Your Love Away

France	Odeon	SO 10132	1965	Picture	'A' Side
France	Odeon	FOS 102	1966	Company	'B' Side
Philippines	Parlophone	PAL 60434	1965	Company	'A' Side

You Can't Do That

You Can't Do That / Can't Buy Me Love

Australia	Parlophone	A8113	1964	Company	'B' Side
Austria	Parlophone	O 28518	1964	Picture	'B' Side
Belgium	Parlophone	R5114	1964	Company	'B' Side
Brazil	EMI	451 3400	19?	Picture	'B' Side
Canada	Capitol	5150	1964	Company	'B' Side
Canada	Capitol	Target 5150	1969/71	Company	'B' Side
Denmark	Parlophone	R5114	1964	Picture	'B' Side
France	Odeon	SO 10111	1964	Picture	'B' Side
Finland	Parlophone	DPY 662	1964	Company	'B' Side
W Germany	Odeon	22 697	1964	Company	'B' Side
India	Parlophone	45-R.5114	1964	Company	'B' Side
Ireland	Parlophone	R (I)5114	1964	Company	'B' Side
Italy	Parlophone	QMSP 16361	1964	Picture	'A' Side
Japan	Apple	AR-1076	1964	Picture	'B' Side
Japan	Odeon	OR-1076	1964	Picture	'B' Side
Japan	Odeon	EAR-20225	1977	Picture	'B' Side
Mexico	Musart	3595	1964	Company	'B' Side
Netherlands	Parlophone	R5114	1964	Company	'B' Side
New Zealand	Parlophone	NZP 3157	1964	Company	'B' Side
Norway	Parlophone	R5114	1964	Picture	'B' Side
Pakistan	Parlophone	R5114	1964	Company	'B' Side
Peru	Odeon	8892	1964	Company	'B' Side
Philippines	Parlophone	PAL 60161	1963	Company	'B' Side
Rhodesia	Parlophone	SPD 304	1964	Company	'B' Side
S Africa	Parlophone	SPD 304	1964	Company	'B' Side
Sweden	Parlophone	R5114	1964	Picture	'B' Side

UK	Parlophone	R5114	1964	Company	'B' Side
USA	Capitol	5150	1964	Picture	'B' Side
USA	Capitol	Target 5150	1969	Company	'B' Side
USA	Capitol J/Box	S7-17690 (Green)	1994-96	Company	'B' Side
W Indies	Capitol	5150	1964	Company	'B' Side

You Know My Name, Look up the Number

You Know My Name, Look up the Number / Let It Be

Australia	Apple	A9083	1970	Picture	'B' Side
Brazil	EMI	45BT 102	19?	Picture	'B' Side
Canada	Apple	2764	1970	Comp. & Pic	'B' Side
Chile	Apple	Apple 13	1970	Company	'B' Side
Denmark	Apple	R5833	1970	Picture	'B' Side
Ecuador	Odeon	87902	1970	Company	'B' Side
France	Apple	2C006-04353	1970	Picture	'B' Side
Greece	Parlophone	GMSP 147	1970	Company	'B' Side
Guatemala	Odeon	4210	1976	Company	'B' Side
W Germany	Apple	1C006-04353	1970	Picture	'B' Side
India	Apple	45-R.5833	1970	Company	'B' Side
Ireland	Apple	R (I)5833	1970	Picture	'B' Side
Israel	Apple	AP 2764	1970	Picture	'B' Side
Italy	Apple	QMSP 16467	1970	Picture	'B' Side
Italy	Apple	3C006-04353	1970	Picture	'B' Side
Japan	Apple	AR-2461	1970	Picture	'B' Side
Japan	Apple	EAR-20242	1977	Picture	'B' Side
Kenya	Parlophone	R 5833	1970	Company	'B' Side
Lebanon	Apple	R5833	1970	Company	'B' Side
Malaysia	Apple	R5833	1970	Company	'B' Side
Mexico	Apple	6645	1970	Picture	'B' Side
Mozambique	Bayal/Parlophone	1 5006	1970	Company	'B' Side

Netherlands	Apple	5C006-04353	1970	Picture	'B' Side
New Zealand	Apple	NZP 3357	1970	Company	'B' Side
Nicaragua	Odeon	O1-0469	1970	Company	'B' Side
Norway	Apple	R5833	1970	Picture	'B' Side
Peru	Apple	10959	1970	Company	'B' Side
Philippines	Apple	PAL 60924	1970	Company	'B' Side
Portugal	Parlophone	8E006-04353	1970	Picture	'B' Side
Rhodesia	Parlophone	SPD 531	1970	Company	'B' Side
S Africa	Parlophone	SPD 531	1970	Company	'B' Side
Singapore	Apple	R5833	1970	Company	'B' Side
Spain	Odeon	1J006-04353	1970	Picture	'B' Side
Sweden	Apple	R5833	1970	Picture	'B' Side
Turkey	Apple	LA 4317	1970	Company	'B' Side
UAR	Parlophone	7041235	1970	Picture	'B' Side
UK	Parlophone	P R 5833	1970	Company	'B' Side
UK	Apple	R5833	1970	Picture	'B' Side
UK	Apple	PR5833	1970	Company	'B' Side
USA	Apple	2764	1970	Picture	'B' Side
USA	Capitol J/Box	S7-17695 (Yellow)	1994-96	Company	'B' Side
Venezuela	Odeon	OD-45-31	1970	Company	'B' Side
W Indies	Parlophone	R5833	1970	Company	'B' Side
Yugoslavia	Apple / Jugoton	SAP 8361	1970	Picture	'B' Side

You Like Me Too Much

You Like Me Too Much / Tell Me What You See

India   Parlophone   45-DPE.185   1965   Company   'A' Side

You Like Me Too Much / The Night Before

Philippines   Parlophone   PAL 60392   1965   Company   'A' Side

You Really Got a Hold on Me

You Really Got a Hold on Me /
I Should Have Known Better

Sweden	Odeon	SD 5971	1964	Picture	'B' Side

You Really Got a Hold on Me /
I Want to Be Your Man

Chile	Odeon	MSOD8525	1965	Picture	'A' Side

You Won't See Me

You Won't See Me / Drive My Car

Philippines	Parlophone	PAL 60470	1966		Company	'B' Side

You Won't See Me / Michelle

India	Parlophone	45-DPE.187	1965		Company	'B' Side
W Indies	Capitol	?	1966		Company	'B' Side

You're Gonna Lose That Girl

You're Gonna Lose That Girl / Dizzy Miss Lizzy

Philippines	Parlophone	PAL 60396	1965	Company	'B' Side

You're Gonna Lose That Girl / Girl

USA	Capitol	4506	1977	Picture	'B' Side

You're Gonna Lose That Girl / Tell Me What You See

Japan	Odeon	OR-1426	1965	Picture	'A' Side
Japan	Apple	AR-1426	1965	Picture	'A' Side
Japan	Odeon	EAS-17063	?	Picture	'A' Side

You've Got to Hide Your Love Away

You've Got to Hide Your Love Away /
I've Just Seen a Face

| USA | Capitol J/Box | S7-18889(Orange) | 1994-96 | Company | 'A' Side |

You've Got to Hide Your Love Away /
The Night Before

| Greece | Parlophone | GMSP 96 | 1965 | Company | 'B' Side |

You've Got to Hide Your Love Away / Yesterday

France	Odeon	SO 10132	1965	Picture	'B' Side
France	Odeon	FOS 102	1966	Company	'A' Side
Philippines	Parlophone	PAL 60434	1965	Company	'B' Side

4. 45 Deccagone Collection 1976

In 1976, 'Decca' decided to issue the 14 songs from the infamous studio audition performed in January 1962, when Pete Best was still the Beatles drummer. There are seven 45 RPM Singles all issued with picture sleeves and all issued in a variety of coloured vinyl. The colours of which are as follows: Blue, Red, Green, Yellow and Crystal.

Three Cool Cats / Hello Little Girl	1100-A
Sheik of Araby / September in the Rain	1101-A
Memphis / Love of the Loved	1102-A
Searching / Like Dreamers Do	1103-A
Sure to Fall / Money	1104-A
Crying, Hoping, Waiting / Till There Was You	1105-A
Besamo Mucho / To Know Him Is to Love Him	1106-A

5. American 'Jukebox' Collection

From 1994 to 1996, Capitol released coloured jukebox 45s, some of the tracks on these records are unique to this collection and can't be found on any other single. So if you're looking for that rarity such as 'Octopus' Garden', this is the place to find it.

These records were issued in a variety of coloured vinyl with a Capitol purple label.

A Hard Day's Night / Things We Said Today	S7-17692-A	White
Across the Universe / Two of Us	S7-18891-A	Crystal
All You Need Is Love / Baby You're a Rich Man	S7-17693-A	Pink
Birthday / Taxman	S7-17488-A	Green or Black
Can't Buy Me Love / You Can't Do That	S7-17690-A	Green
Got to Get You into My Life / Helter Skelter	S7-18899-A	Orange
Help / I'm Down	S7-17691-A	White
Here Comes the Sun / Octopus' Garden	S7-17700-A	Orange
Here, There and Everywhere / Good Day Sunshine	S7-18897-A	Orange
Hey Jude / Revolution	S7-17694-A	Blue
I Want to Hold Your Hand / This Boy	S7-17689-A	Crystal
It's All Too Much / Only a Northern Song	S7-18893-A	Blue
Let It Be / You Know My Name	S7-17695-A	Yellow
Love Me Do / PS I Love You	S7-56785-A	Red or Black
Lucy in the Sky with Diamonds / When I'm Sixty-Four	S7-18896-A	Red
Magical Mystery Tour / The Fool on the Hill	S7-18890-A	Yellow
Norwegian Wood / If I Needed Someone	S7-18888-A	Green or Black
Norwegian Wood / If I Needed Someone	S7-19341-A	Green or Black
Nowhere Man / What Goes On	S7-18894-A	Green
Ob-La-Di, Ob-La-Da / Julia	S7-18900-A	Crystal
Paperback Writer / Rain	S7-18902-A	Red
Sgt Pepper with a Little Help / A Day in the Life	S7-17701-A	Crystal

She Loves You / I'll Get You	S7-17688-A	Red
Something / Come Together	S7-17698-A	Blue
Strawberry Fields / Penny Lane	S7-17697-A	Red
The Long and Winding Road / For You Blue	S7-18898-A	Blue
Twist and Shout / There's a Place	S7-17699-A	Pink
While My Guitar Gentle Weeps / Blackbird	S7-18892-A	Blue
Yesterday / Act Naturally	S7-18901-A	Pink
You've Got to Hide Your Love / I've Just Seen a Face	S7-18889-A	Green

All the records listed above are included in the 45-RPM section under their individual titles.

6. <u>Polydor 331/3 Singles</u>

As far as I am aware, there were only two Polydor singles ever released throughout the world at 331/3 RPM. These were all manufactured and issued in Argentina, as listed below. If anyone should know of any others, I would grateful for any information on them.

Ain't She Sweet

Ain't She Sweet /
Take out Some Insurance on Me

Argentina	Polydor	25-077	1964	Company	'A' Side

My Bonnie

My Bonnie / The Saints

Argentina	Polydor	25-048	1964	Company	'A' Side

Take out Some Insurance on Me

Take out Some Insurance on Me / Ain't She Sweet

Argentina	Polydor	25-077	1964	Company	'B' Side

The Saints

The Saints / My Bonnie

Argentina	Polydor	25-048	1964	Company	'B' Side

7. 331/3 RPM Singles

Whilst most countries in the world preferred to produce singles at a speed of 45 RPM, there were some who produced and issued singles at 331/3 RPM. I do not know the reasoning behind this, but perhaps some knowledgeable record collector will enlighten my good self on the subject.

I have found, to date, only five countries that produced and issued Beatles' singles at 331/3 RPM.

These are in alphabetical order, as follows:

1. Argentina
2. Bolivia
3. Brazil
4. Costa Rica
5. Uruguay

These records covered 76 different titles with 46 compilations, all released on the Odeon or Apple label.

331/3 RPM Singles

Titles

A Hard Day's Night

A Hard Day's Night /
I Should Have Known Better

Brazil	Odeon	71 30 83	1964	Picture	'A' Side

A Hard Day's Night / Long Tall Sally

Argentina	Odeon Pops	DTOA 3274	1964	Picture	'A' Side
Uruguay	Odeon Pops	DTOA 3274	1964	Company	'A' Side

A Hard Day's Night / Things We Said Today

Costa Rica	Odeon	25058	1964	Company	'A' Side

A Taste of Honey

A Taste of Honey / Misery

Costa Rica	Odeon	25081	1965	Company	'B' Side

All My Loving

All My Loving / Please Mr. Postman

Argentina	Odeon Popa	DTOA 3217	1964	Picture	'A' Side

All You Need Is Love

All You Need Is Love / Baby You're a Rich Man

Argentina	Odeon Pops	DTOA 8312	1967	Company	'B' Side
Brazil	Odeon	7-BT-06	1967	Picture	'A' Side
Uruguay	Odeon	3540	1967	Company	'B' Side

Any Time at All

Any Time at All / I'll Cry Instead

Costa Rica	Odeon	25059	1964	Company	'B' Side

Baby You're a Rich Man

Baby You're a Rich Man / All You Need Is Love

Argentina	Odeon Pops	DTOA 8312	1967	Company	'A' Side
Brazil	Odeon	7-BT-06	1967	Picture	'B' Side
Uruguay	Odeon	3540	1967	Company	'A' Side

Birthday

Birthday / Honey Pie

Argentina	Apple	DTOA 8498	1969	Picture?	'A' Side

Boys

Boys / Money

Argentina	Odeon Pops	DTOA 3249	1964	Picture	'A' Side

Can't Buy Me Love

Can't Buy Me Love / You Can't Do That

Argentina	Odeon Pops	DTOA 3220	1964	Picture	'A' Side

Come Together

Come Together / Something

Argentina	Apple	DTOA 8539	1970	Company	'A' Side
Brazil	Apple	7-BT-26	1969	Company	'B' Side

Day Tripper

Day Tripper / We Can Work It Out

Argentina	Odeon Pops	DTOA 8137	1966	Company	'B' Side
Brazil	Odeon	7-BT-01	1966	Picture	'A' Side
Bolivia	Odeon	7-BT-01	1965	Picture	'A' Side

Dear Prudence

Dear Prudence / Ob-La-Di, Ob-La-Da

Brazil	Odeon	DP 412	1968	Picture	'B' Side

Devil in Her Heart

Devil in Her Heart / Roll Over Beethoven

Argentina	Odeon Pops	DTOA 3218	1964	Picture	'B' Side

Devil in Her Heart / She Loves You

Costa Rica	Odeon	25071	1964	Company	'B' Side

Don't Let Me Down

Don't Let Me Down / Get Back

Argentina	Apple	DTOA 8483	1969	Company	'B' Side
Brazil	Apple	7-BT-17	1969	Picture	'A' Side
Uruguay	Apple	30003	1969	Company	'B' Side

Eight Days a Week

Eight Days a Week / No Reply

Costa Rica	Odeon	25076	1965	Company	'A' Side

Eight Days a Week / Rock and Roll Music

Argentina	Odeon Pops	DTOA 8021	1965	Picture	'A' Side
Brazil	Odeon	71 3119	1965	Picture	'A' Side
Bolivia	Odeon	BO-1040	1965	Company	'A' Side

Eleanor Rigby

Eleanor Rigby / Yellow Submarine

Argentina	Odeon Pops	DTOA 8213	1966	Picture	'B' Side
Brazil	Odeon	7-BT-04	1966	Picture	'B' Side
Uruguay	Odeon	3495	1966	Company	'A' Side

For You Blue

For You Blue / The Long and Winding Road

Argentina	Apple	DTOA 8617	1970	Picture	'B' Side
Brazil	Apple	7-BT-37	1970	Picture	'B' Side

From Me to You

From Me to You / Please, Please Me

Brazil	Odeon	71 3044	1963	Picture	'B' Side

From Me to You / Thank You Girl

Argentina	Odeon Pops	DTOA 3125	1963	Company	'A' Side

Get Back

Get Back / Don't Let Me Down

Argentina	Apple	DTOA 8483	1969	Company	'A' Side
Brazil	Apple	7-BT-17	1969	Picture	'B' Side
Uruguay	Apple	30003	1969	Company	'A' Side

Hello, Goodbye

Hello, Goodbye / I Am the Walrus

Argentina	Odeon Pops	DTOA 8364	1967	Company	'A' Side
Brazil	Odeon	7-BT-08	1967	Picture	'A' Side
Uruguay	Odeon	3557	1967	Company	'A' Side

Help

Help / I'm Down

Argentina	Odeon Pops	DTOA 8072	1965	Picture	'A' Side
Bolivia	Odeon Pops	7-BT-04	1965	Company	'A' Side
Uruguay	Odeon	3417	1965	Company	'A' Side

Hey Jude

Hey Jude / Revolution

Argentina	Odeon Pops	DTOA 8427	1968	Company	'A' Side
Brazil	Odeon	7-BT-12	1968	Picture	'A' Side
Bolivia	Odeon Pops	BO-1158	1968	Company	'A' Side
Uruguay	Odeon	20005	1968	Company	'A' Side

Honey Don't

Honey Don't / I'll Follow the Sun

Argentina	Odeon	DTOA 8028	1965	Picture	'A' Side

Honey Pie

Honey Pie / Birthday

Argentina	Apple	DTOA 8498	1969	Picture?	'B' Side

I Am the Walrus

I Am the Walrus / Hello, Goodbye

Argentina	Odeon Pops	DTOA 8364	1967	Company	'B' Side
Brazil	Odeon	7-BT-08	1967	Picture	'B' Side
Uruguay	Odeon	3557	1967	Company	'B' Side

I Feel Fine

I Feel Fine / If I Fell

Brazil	Odeon	71 3102	1965	Picture	'A' Side

I Feel Fine / She's a Woman

Argentina	Odeon Pops	DTOA 3279	1965	Picture	'A' Side

I Saw Her Standing There

I Saw Her Standing There / Twist and Shout

Argentina	Odeon Pops	DTOA 3197	1964	Picture	'B' Side

I Should Have Known Better

I Should Have Known Better /
A Hard Day's Night

| Brazil | Odeon | 71 30 83 | 1964 | Picture | 'B' Side |

I Should Have Known Better / I'll Cry Instead

| Argentina | Odeon Pops | Dtoa 8030 | 1965 | Picture | 'A' Side |

I Want to Be Your Man

I Want to Be Your Man / Not a Second Time

| Costa Rica | Odeon | 25037 | 1964 | Company | 'A' Side |

I Want to Hold Your Hand

I Want to Hold Your Hand / She Loves You

| Brazil | Odeon | 71 3049 | 1964 | Picture | 'A' Side |

I Want to Hold Your Hand / This Boy

| Argentina | Odeon Pops | DTOA 3186 | 1964 | Company | 'A' Side |

If I Fell

If I Fell / I Feel Fine

Brazil	Odeon	71 3102	1965	Picture	'A' Side

I'll Cry Instead

I'll Cry Instead / Any Time at All

Costa Rica	Odeon	25059	1964	Company	'A' Side

I'll Cry Instead / I Should Have Known Better

Argentina	Odeon Pops	DTOA 8030	1965	Company	'B' Side

I'll Follow the Sun

I'll Follow the Sun / Honey Don't

Argentina	Odeon	DTOA 8028	1965	Picture	'B' Side

I'll Get You

I'll Get You / She Loves You

| Argentina | Odeon Pops | DTOA 3185 | 1964 | Company | 'B' Side |
| Uruguay | Odeon | 3376 | 1964 | Company | 'B' Side |

I'm Down

I'm Down / Help

Argentina	Odeon Pops	DTOA 8072	1965	Picture	'B' Side
Bolivia	Odeon Pops	7-BT-04	1965	Company	'B' Side
Uruguay	Odeon	3417	1965	Company	'B' Side

Kansas City

Kansas City / Words of Love

| Costa Rica | Odeon | 25074 | 1965 | Company | 'B' Side |

Lady Madonna

Lady Madonna / The Inner Light

Argentina	Odeon Pops	DTOA 8389	1968	Picture	'A' Side
Brazil	Odeon	7-BT-09	1968	Picture	'A' Side
Uruguay	Odeon	20001	1968	Company	'A' Side

Let It Be

Let It Be / You Know My Name

Argentina	Apple	8556	1970	Picture	'A' Side
Brazil	Apple	7-BT-31	1970	Picture	'A' Side
Uruguay	Apple	30011	1970	Company	'A' Side

Let It Be / Across the Universe

Russia	Memoanr	M62-36715	19?	Company	'A' Side

Long Tall Sally

Long Tall Sally / A Hard Day's Night

Argentina	Odeon Pops	DTOA 3274	1964	Picture	'B' Side
Uruguay	Odeon Pops	DTOA 3274	1964	Company	'B' Side

Long Tall Sally / I Call Your Name

Brazil	Odeon	71 3074	1964	Picture	'A' Side

Love Me Do

Love Me Do / Please, Please Me

Argentina	Odeon Pops	DTOA 3169	1963	Company	'B' Side
Uruguay	Odeon	3376	1963	Company	'B' Side

Michelle

Michelle / Nowhere Man

| Argentina | Odeon Pops | DTOA 3274 | 1966 | Picture | 'A' Side |

Michelle / Yesterday

| Brazil | Odeon | 7-BT-03 | 1966 | Picture | 'A' Side |

Misery

Misery / A Taste of Honey

| Costa Rica | Odeon | 25081 | 1965 | Company | 'A' Side |

Money

Money / Boys

| Argentina | Odeon Pops | DTOA 3249 | 1964 | Picture | 'B' Side |

No Reply

No Reply / Eight Days a Week

| Costa Rica | Odeon | 25076 | 1965 | Company | 'B' Side |

Not a Second Time

Not a Second Time / I Want to Be Your Man

Costa Rica	Odeon	25037	1964	Company	'B' Side

Nowhere Man

Nowhere Man / Michelle

Argentina	Odeon Pops	DTOA 3274	1966	Picture	'B' Side

Ob-La-Da, Ob-La-Di

Ob-La-Di, Ob-La-Da / Dear Prudence

Brazil	Odeon	DP 412	1968	Picture	'A' Side

Ob-La-Di, Ob-La-Da / While My Guitar Gently Weeps

Argentina	Apple	DTOA 8475	1969	Company	'A' Side
Brazil	Apple	7-BT-16	1969	Picture	'A' Side

Old Brown Shoe

Old Brown Shoe / The Ballad of John and Yoko

Argentina	Apple	DTOA 8486	1969	Company	'B' Side
Brazil	Apple	7-BT-21	1969	Picture	'B' Side
Uruguay	Apple	30005	1969	Company	'B' Side

Paperback Writer

Paperback Writer / Rain

Argentina	Odeon Pops	DTOA 8191	1966	Picture	'A' Side
Brazil	Odeon	7-BT-02	1966	Picture	'A' Side
Uruguay	Odeon	3460	1966	Company	'A' Side

Penny Lane

Penny Lane / Strawberry Fields

Argentina	Odeon Pops	DTOA 8260	1967	Company	'B' Side
Brazil	Odeon	7-BT-05	1967	Picture	'B' Side
Uruguay	Odeon	3530	1967	Company	'B' Side

Please Mr. Postman

Please Mr. Postman / All My Loving

Argentina	Odeon Pops	DTOA 3217	1964	Picture	'B' Side

Please, Please Me

Please, Please Me / Love Me Do

Argentina	Odeon Pops	DTOA 3169	1963	Company	'A' Side
Uruguay	Odeon	3376	1963	Company	'A' Side

Please, Please Me / From Me to You

Brazil	Odeon	71 3044	1963	Picture	'A' Side

Rain

Rain / Paperback Writer

Argentina	Odeon Pops	DTOA 8191	1966	Picture	'B' Side
Brazil	Odeon	7-BT-02	1966	Picture	'B' Side
Uruguay	Odeon	3460	1966	Company	'A' Side

Revolution

Revolution / Hey Jude

Argentina	Odeon Pops	DTOA 8427	1968	Company	'B' Side
Brazil	Odeon	7-BT-12	1968	Picture	'B' Side
Bolivia	Odeon Pops	BO-1158	1968	Company	'B' Side
Uruguay	Odeon	20005	1968	Company	'B' Side

Rock and Roll Music

Rock and Roll Music / Eight Days a Week

Argentina	Odeon Pops	DTOA 8021	1965	Picture	'B' Side
Brazil	Odeon	71 3119	1965	Picture	'B' Side
Bolivia	Odeon	BO-1040	1965	Company	'B' Side

Roll Over Beethoven

Roll Over Beethoven / Devil in Her Heart

Argentina	Odeon Pops	DTOA 3218	1964	Picture	'A' Side

She Loves You

She Loves You / Devil in Her Heart

Costa Rica	Odeon	25071	1964	Picture	'A' Side

She Loves You / I'll Get You

Argentina	Odeon Pops	DTOA 3185	1964	Company	'A' Side
Uruguay	Odeon	3376	1964	Company	'A' Side

She Loves You / I Want to Hold Your Hand

Brazil	Odeon	71 3049	1964	Picture	'B' Side

She's a Woman

She's a Woman / I Feel Fine

Argentina	Odeon Pops	DTOA 3279	1965	Picture	'B' Side

Something

Something / Come Together

Argentina	Apple	DTOA 8539	1970	Company	'B' Side
Brazil	Apple	7-BT-26	1969	Company	'A' Side

Strawberry Fields

Strawberry Fields / Penny Lane

Argentina	Odeon Pops	DTOA 8260	1967	Company	'A' Side
Brazil	Odeon	7-BT-05	1967	Picture	'A' Side
Uruguay	Odeon	3530	1967	Company	'A' Side

Thank You Girl

Thank You Girl / From Me to You

Argentina	Odeon Pops	DTOA 3125	1963	Company	'B' Side

The Ballad of John and Yoko

The Ballad of John and Yoko / Old Brown Shoe

Argentina	Apple	DTOA 8486	1969	Company	A' Side
Brazil	Apple	7-BT-21	1969	Picture	'A' Side
Uruguay	Apple	30005	1969	Company	'A' Side

The Inner Light

The Inner Light / Lady Madonna

Argentina	Odeon Pops	DTOA 8389	1968	Picture	'B' Side
Brazil	Odeon	7-BT-09	1968	Picture	'B' Side
Uruguay	Odeon	20001	1968	Company	'B' Side

The Long and Winding Road

The Long and Winding Road / For You Blue

Argentina	Apple	DTOA 8617	1970	Picture	'A' Side
Brazil	Apple	7-BT-37	1970	Picture	'A' Side

Things We Said Today

Things We Said Today / A Hard Day's Night

Costa Rica	Odeon	25058	1964	Company	'B' Side

This Boy

This Boy / I Want to Hold Your Hand

| Argentina | Odeon Pops | DTOA 3186 | 1964 | Company | 'B' Side |

This Boy / Ticket to Ride

| Brazil | Odeon | 71 3134 | 1965 | Picture | 'B' Side |

Ticket to Ride

Ticket to Ride / This Boy

| Brazil | Odeon | 71 3134 | 1965 | Picture | 'A' Side |

Ticket to Ride / Yes It Is

| Argentina | Odeon Pops | DTOA 8043 | 1965 | Picture | 'A' Side |

Twist and Shout

Twist and Shout / I Saw Her Standing There

| Argentina | Odeon Pops | DTOA 3197 | 1964 | Picture | 'A' Side |

We Can Work It Out

We Can Work It Out / Day Tripper

| Argentina | Odeon Pops | DTOA 8137 | 1966 | Company | 'A' Side |
| Brazil | Odeon | 7-BT-01 | 1966 | Picture | 'B' Side |

While My Guitar Gently Weeps

While My Guitar Gently Weeps / Ob-La-Di, Ob-La-Da

| Argentina | Apple | DTOA 8475 | 1969 | Company | 'B' Side |
| Brazil | Apple | 7-BT-16 | 1969 | Picture | 'B' Side |

Words of Love

Words of Love Kansas City

| Costa Rica | Odeon | 25074 | 1965 | Company | 'A' Side |

Yellow Submarine

Yellow Submarine / Eleanor Rigby

Argentina	Odeon Pops	DTOA 8213	1966	Picture	'A' Side
Brazil	Odeon	7-BT-04	1966	Picture	'A' Side
Uruguay	Odeon	3495	1966	Company	'B' Side

Yes It Is

Yes It Is / Ticket to Ride

Argentina	Odeon Pops	DTOA 8043	1965	Picture	'A' Side

Yesterday

Yesterday / Michelle

Brazil	Odeon	7-BT-03	1966	Picture	'B' Side

You Can't Do That

You Can't Do That / Can't Buy Me Love

Argentina	Odeon Pops	DTOA 3220	1964	Picture	'B' Side

You Know My Name

You Know My Name / Let It Be

Argentina	Apple	8556	1970	Picture	'B' Side
Brazil	Apple	7-BT-31	1970	Picture	'B' Side
Uruguay	Apple	30011	1970	Company	'B' Side

8. The First 78 Single and the Last 45

In 1958, John Lennon's group, known as 'The Quarrymen', made up of John Lennon, Paul McCartney, George Harrison and three other members, decided to make a 'demo' record. In those days, there were individual, small, one-man studios that would be willing to undertake the recording of a vinyl disc for a small fee. One such studio was the front room of an old Victorian house in Kensington Street, Liverpool, owned by one Percy Phillips who for the princely sum 12s 6d (88p in modern currency) would undertake the task.

The Quarrymen paid the necessary fee and proceeded to record a cover version of Buddy Hollies song 'That'll Be the Day' and on the flip side was a song called 'In Spite of All the Danger', the latter being composed by Paul McCartney and George Harrison. This was recorded on a 78-RPM disc and was consequently passed, in turn, around all the members of the group and was finally passed into obscurity, long forgotten.

In the late nineties, a member of the original Quarrymen, who still had the record in his possession and who had come on hard times, decided to sell the disc, offering it to one of the reputable 'pop' memorability sales companies, wondering what value it had, if any. They contacted Paul McCartney to authenticate it and as a result, he purchased it privately for an undisclosed sum. Rumour has it was in the million-pound region, making it one of the rarest and most valuable records of all time.

He, consequently, had the record professionally restored and had a limited amount of copies made on 45-RPM 7" discs, these he distributed to the Beatles' close families and associates. These 45s, because of their rarity, would command a very high value in this day and age.

Hence, we have the first 78 and consequently the last 45 record of the Beatles, albeit only three of them contributed to the contents.